WHO IS THIS JESUS WHO DIED FOR YOU?

AUBREY L. DUNCAN

WHO IS THIS JESUS WHO DIED FOR YOU?

All Rights Reserved © 2017 by Aubrey L. Duncan

Printed in the United States of America
Library of Congress Control Number: 2016905457
ISBN: 978-0-9749490-4-8

Cover Design by Rob Wilson

Published by
Advent Truth Ministries, Inc.
Forsyth, GA 31029
www.adventtruth.org

Dedication:
To all who love Jesus
and want to be saved in
His Soon-Coming Kingdom

INTRODUCTION

*T*oday, there is a clarion call in the faith community for all religions to come together for the purpose of fostering world peace. Recognizing the conflicts, rifts, and mistrust among the several factions, the promoters of this coming-together movement feel that greater peace can be achieved if all religions become united. Essentially, the argument put forth is that if each faith group, by casting aside their peculiar points of doctrines, they can unite and ushering in a season of universal peace. Its promoters conclude that, at the very core of spirituality, they all worship the same god and would thus find salvation through whomever each group recognizes as its god.

Their efforts have come to be known as the Ecumenical Movement. It began with the Christian community seeking to find common ground on which to work together for proclamation of the Christian Gospel. "Let's put aside our differences", its leaders claimed, "so that we can reach more people for Christ". That movement has now spread beyond Christendom to include, Islam, Hinduism, Buddhism, Shintoism, and just about every other religion known to humanity. This movement is built on an elusive and misunderstood concept called 'love'. It is certainly not the love that was demonstrated by the Only True God in the person of His Only Begotten Son, Jesus Christ.

The line of thinking of the Ecumenical Movement places the sincere Christian in a real predicament; for the apostle Peter fervently affirmed, "Neither is there salvation in any other: for there is none other name under heaven, given among men whereby we must be saved" (Acts 4:12). This is the most peculiar doctrine of the Christian faith. Such being the case; how can a true Christian become part of the rapidly metastasizing Ecumenical Movement? To do so would be to deny who truly Jesus is. Either one would have to abandon their Christian faith or be prepared to endure the ridicule, criticism, and rejection by the movement. It's a personal decision each one who calls himself/herself a Christian will have to make. Groupthink will not suffice.

Men have debated, discussed, and even denied who Jesus truly is. But who really is this Jesus, anyway? Was He just a good man? Was He simply another charismatic and influential religious teacher? Was He a fraud and cosmic trickster? Or, Was He God as He claimed, and His followers believed Him to be?

This volume answers those and other questions that will edify you and strengthen your faith in Jesus Christ. It looks at His many attributes and presents the evidence of Jesus Christ being exactly whom He claims to be--the Messiah, the Only Savior of the world.

TABLE OF CONTENTS

Chapter 1

THE ONLY ONE

*S*tories are powerful building blocks for nation development. They are critical catalysts for societal changes and potent instruments for character transformation. Take for example the greatest story ever told, the story of Jesus Christ. The story of His virgin birth, His sinless life, His sacrificial death on Calvary's cross, His bodily resurrection His mediational ministry in the heavenly sanctuary, and His soon coming as King of kings and Lord of lords has served not only to build a great nation (Christianity); but it has impacted societies around the world like none other has. His story has undoubtedly transformed more characters than any legal concept ever implemented or political device conceived.

The way in which we measure historical time is rooted in His death, burial and resurrection, or passion, as it is generally referred to. Jesus himself, recognizing the power of a good story to alter men's lives, change the course of nations and restructure societies, used them liberally to help His hearers better understand who He was and what His mission entailed. The theme of His story has resounded across more cultures than any other story known to humanity. Its structure transcends national and international boundaries. The story of Jesus Christ evokes love, power, and awe. It's a story of the most precious, abundant, and amazing love the world will ever know. His is the greatest story ever told.

Take for example, Christmastime. None can avoid the sentiment of that season. There is the gift-giving. Carols are playing and families are gathering together for celebrations. The atmosphere is deluged with the fragrance of joy. Regardless of your theological opinion or religious persuasion, it is virtually impossible not to be impacted by the life and ministry of this Galilean itinerant preacher. He entered upon the stage of life's drama some two thousand years ago and has left an indelible signature that has forever altered the course of human history.

According to the Holy Bible, salvation is defined as the restoration of God's image in humanity. The sacred record reveals that God created man in His [God's] image. The prophet Moses writes, "And God said, Let **Us** make man in our image, after our likeness: and let them have dominion over the fish of the sea, and over the fowl of the air, and over the cattle, and over all the earth, and over every creeping thing that creepeth upon the earth...So God created man in his own image, in the image of God created he him; male and female created he them" (Genesis 1:26-27).

But who was this '**Us**' that was speaking at creation? Jesus Christ answers affirmatively. In His last recorded prayer, Jesus Christ prayed to His Father, "That they all may be one; as thou, Father, art in me, and I in thee, that they also may be one in **Us**: that the world may believe that thou hast sent Me" (John 17:21). Ironically, this very passage of Scripture is used by the Ecumenical Movement to justify all religions coming together as they abandon the distinctive features of their particular faiths.

And what is the image of God in which man was created? When Moses asked God to show him [Moses] His [God's] glory, God proclaimed, "The Lord, the Lord God, merciful and gracious, longsuffering, and abundant in goodness and truth" (Exodus 34:6). The Psalmist David agrees, "The Lord is merciful and gracious, slow to anger, and plenteous in mercy (Psalm 103:8). These are the inherent qualities of God's character. It is the image in which man was created. The Bible is replete with this image of God. But something happened that caused man to lose those qualities and thereby mar God's image in him. The Bible calls that thing 'sin'. It is thus described, "Whosoever committeth sin transgresseth also the law: for sin is the transgression of the law" (1 John 3:4). It was what the first human beings, Adam and Eve, did when they chose to go against God's command to them.

We are told, "Man was originally endowed with noble powers and a well-balanced mind. He was perfect in his being, and in harmony with God. His thoughts were pure, his aims holy. But through disobedience, his powers were perverted, and selfishness took the place of love. His nature became so weakened through transgression that it was impossible for him, in his own strength, to resist the power of evil. He was made captive by Satan, and would have remained so forever had not God specially interposed. It was the tempter's purpose to thwart the divine plan in man's creation, and fill the earth with woe and desolation. And he would point to all this evil as the result of God's work in creating man" (Steps to Christ, E.G. White, pg. 16).

God's law is verily the reflection of His character of righteousness and His standard by which He requires all humanity to live. David again admonishes us, "Thy righteousness is an everlasting righteousness, and thy law is the truth... My tongue shall speak of thy word: for all thy commandments are righteousness" (Psalm 119:142,172).

Beginning with the first created humans to the very day in which we live, none, except Jesus Christ, has been able to perfectly keep God's law, and thus fully reflect His image. Therefore, the apostle Paul was able to conclude, "For all have sinned, and come short of the glory of God" (Romans 3:23). His glory refers to His character. Jesus explains, "And now, O Father, glorify thou me with thine own self with the glory which I had with thee before the world was" (John 17:5).

Because of God's love, graciousness, goodness, and mercy; verily because of who He is, Jesus exclaimed, "For God so loved the world, that he gave his only begotten Son, that whosoever believeth in him should not perish, but have everlasting life" (John 3:16). In other words, through Jesus Christ, and Him alone, can the image of God be restored to man. This is the only true way to salvation. The angel announced to Joseph, "And she [Mary, his espoused wife] shall bring forth a son, and thou shalt call his name Jesus: for He shall save his people from their sins" (Matthew 1:21).

The prophet Isaiah was able to predict with divine precision, the work that Jesus Christ was to perform. He declared, "For unto us a child is born, unto us a son is given: and the government shall be upon his shoulder: and his name shall be called Wonderful, Counsellor, The mighty God, The everlasting Father, The Prince of Peace" (Isaiah 9:6).

As one studies the life of Jesus, it is plain to see that indeed the prophet's words are most applicable. His cruel death on Calvary's cross was the epitome of that life of pain and suffering.

Called by God to deliver a stern message of judgement to his countrymen in Jerusalem, the prophet Micah did not flinch from pointing out the apostasy of his countrymen who were oppressing the poor and abusing those less fortunate. He warned them of God's judgement to come. But then, he held out God's promise of restoration by sending the promised Messiah. Micah assured them, "But thou, Bethlehem Ephratah, though thou be little among the thousands of Judah, yet out of thee shall he come forth unto me that is to be ruler in Israel; whose goings forth have been from of old, from everlasting" (Micah 5:2). He, in fact, prophesied of the exact place of Jesus' birth even as he reminded his countrymen that Jesus was from everlasting.

Interestingly, Jesus' parents did not live in Bethlehem. Nazareth, a small insignificant village some 90 miles away, was their residence. His mother Mary was nine months pregnant with her baby Jesus when the Roman Emperor, Caesar Augustus, decreed that all in the empire should be counted and taxed. In order to accomplish this, each family had to travel to the city of their lineage according to their tribe. Being of the tribe of Judah and lineage of David, the residents of Nazareth, including Joseph and Mary, had to make the journey to Bethlehem, the city of David to be counted and taxed. Just as was prophesied by Micah, Jesus was born in Bethlehem. The angels announced to the shepherds, "Fear not: for, behold, I bring you good tidings of great joy, which shall be to all people. For unto you is born this day in the city of David a Saviour, which is Christ the Lord" (Luke 2:10-11). This was no mere coincidence. His birth occurred precisely as prophesied hundreds of years before the event.

In addition to accurately prophesizing the time, place, and manner of His birth, the ancient seers also accurately foretold the time that Jesus Christ would begin His earthly ministry, when it would end, and the time He would die. The prophet Daniel, while in Babylonian captivity some six hundred years before Jesus' birth, gave this strikingly detailed account of those events. He related, "Seventy weeks are determined upon thy people and upon thy holy city, to finish the transgression, and to make an end of sins, and to make reconciliation for iniquity, and to bring in everlasting righteousness, and to seal up the vision and prophecy, and to anoint the Most Holy. Know therefore and understand, that from the going forth of the commandment to restore and to build Jerusalem unto the Messiah the Prince shall be seven weeks, and threescore and two weeks: the street shall be built again, and the wall, even in troublous times. And after threescore and two weeks shall Messiah be cut off, but not for himself" (Daniel 9:24-26).

Exactly at the time prophesied, Jesus began His ministry. Speaking in the synagogue in His hometown of Nazareth, on the Sabbath-day, He declared, "The Spirit of the Lord is upon me, because he hath anointed me to preach the gospel to the poor; he hath sent me to heal the brokenhearted, to preach deliverance to the captives, and recovering of sight to the blind, to set at liberty them that are bruised, To preach the acceptable year of the Lord...This day is this scripture fulfilled in your ears" (Luke 4:16-21). He was in fact quoting the prophecy of the prophet Isaiah spoken more than six hundred years earlier (Isaiah 61:1-2). His earthly ministry lasted for exactly the time as was prophesied by Daniel. It began in fall of 27AD. He was crucified 3 ½ years later in the Spring of 30AD.

So convincing is this revelation and fulfillment of who Jesus Christ really is, the promised Messiah and Only Savior of the world, that the leaders who rejected Him pronounced a curse upon anyone who would study and understand this sacred truth. The curse reads, "May the bones of the fingers decay and decompose, of him who turns the pages of the Book of Daniel, to find out the time of Daniel (9:24-27), and may his memory rot from off the face of the earth forever" (Talmudic Law, page 978, section 2, line 28). Why should such a stern pronouncement be necessary? Simply because this prophecy, above all others, prove beyond the shadow of any doubt that the Jesus whom they rejected and nailed to the cruel cross of Calvary was none other than the Messiah whom they claimed to be looking forward to.

Despite such threatenings, there were those who not only recognized; but accepted Jesus Christ for who He truly is. John the Baptist, when asked by those very leaders that would eventually crucify the Savior, who he (John the Baptist) was, referred them to the writings of the seer Isaiah. He informed them, "I am the voice of one crying in the wilderness, Make straight the way of the Lord, as said the prophet Esaias" (Isaiah 40:3, John 1:23). Isaiah also prophesied that Jesus would be the Light to those that walk in darkness: "The people that walked in darkness have seen a great light: they that dwell in the land of the shadow of death, upon them hath the light shined"(Isaiah 9:2). So, Jesus himself would later declare, "I am the Light of the world: he that followeth me shall not walk in darkness, but shall have the light of life" (John 8:12).

We have this historical account from one who was not a follower of Jesus; but nevertheless, obviously recognized Him for who He is. In Rome, in the year 93, the Jewish historian, Josephus, published his lengthy history of the Jews. While discussing the period in which the Jews of Judaea were governed by the Roman procurator Pontius Pilate, Josephus included the following account: "About this time there lived Jesus, a wise man, if indeed one ought to call him a man. For he was one who performed surprising deeds and was a teacher of such people as accept the truth gladly. He won over many Jews and many of the Greeks. He was the Messiah. And when, upon the accusation of the principal men among us, Pilate had condemned him to a cross, those who had first come to love him did not cease. He appeared to them spending a third day restored to life, for the prophets of God had foretold these things and a thousand other marvels about him. And the tribe of the Christians, so called after him, has still to this day not disappeared" (Jewish Antiquities, 18.3.3 §63).

A modern day disciple observed, "Some skeptics have suggested that these prophecies were accidentally or coincidently fulfilled by Jesus. According to the

Science of Probability, the chance of any one human being-up until the present-fulfilling a selection of just 8 of these prophecies (including the one on the crucifixion) is 1 in 10^{17}...And here we are considering only 8 prophecies. What if we were to consider 48 prophecies? The chance then becomes virtually zero. (1 in 10^{157}). That's like finding a particular grain of sand out of all the sand on earth and beneath the sea. What about all 61 prophecies?" (Evidence that demands a verdict, Josh Mc Dowell).

Despite claims to the contrary, Jesus Christ is the only way of salvation. He makes it abundantly plain, "Verily, verily, I say unto you, I am the door of the sheep. All that ever came before me are thieves and robbers: but the sheep did not hear them. I am the door: by me if any man enter in, he shall be saved, and shall go in and out, and find pasture. The thief cometh not, but for to steal, and to kill, and to destroy: I am come that they might have life, and that they might have it more abundantly" (John 10:7-10).

Not only is Jesus the Messiah, the Only Savior of the world; but He is the Only Mediator and Intercessor between God and man. The apostle Paul informs us, "For there is one God, and one mediator between God and men, the man Christ Jesus" (1 Timothy 2:5).

He is indeed the Only One--the One who died for you.

Chapter 2

GOD WITH US

$\mathcal{A}$ll religions are essentially based on one fundamental principle--the need for eternal life. Fact is, no one ever wants to die. Even the ones that commit suicide do so only because they feel they have no other choice, no other hope; but certainly not because they seek death for death's sake. Of all the religions known to the human family, only one can claim the certainty of eternal life.

This is a claim substantiated by more than faith or mere religious dogma. It is demonstrated by the God who has done that which no other god has done--- became like unto His servants, died for them, resurrected Himself and assures them that He will come again to be with them eternally. The song writer declared, 'How great thou art'. He is God with us.

Every member of humanity has a god. Whether one is a member of an organized religious sect, claims to experience a higher power on their own, or professes to be an atheist, the undeniable fact is that they all believe in a god. By definition, a god is a power beyond our natural realm in which one finds purpose for his/her being. For most, that god is a being possessing more than human attributes. For others, it simply may be another human being whom they look upon as superior to themselves and anyone else they can think of. For those who claim that there is no god, they in effect create a god out of their belief that there is no god.

Still others, believe in a God who is the ruler of the vast, boundless and unfathomable universe. They believe that He created and rules over the entire universe, from the minutest atom to the most majestic star. They believe that He provides for their every need and has His hand not only in their personal lives; but throughout the full spectrum of the human experience.

The Holy Bible, the sacred text of the Christian faith, presents such a God. Not only does it portray a God of omnipotence, omniscience, omnipresence; it tells of a God who loves his subjects so much that he stepped out of His sphere of illimitable space and boundless time to become one of them and lived among them. He characterizes himself as a God who understands the condition of every soul and can satisfy the yearning of every human heart. He, in fact, is depicted as the Only True God, the God of all humanity. Of the many names which are accorded Him, the most well-known is also the most controversial. That name is Jesus Christ.

Whatever one thinks about Him, the one undeniable fact about Him is that He did sojourn with the human family in like fashion as we are. More convincingly, are the hundreds of predictions about Him that have been fulfilled with uncanny accuracy and flawless precision.

When He walked on planet earth, the religious leaders of His nation were in constant debate with Him as to who He really was. On one such occasion, Jesus Christ directed them to the writings of their own forefathers so that they can discover who He truly is. He admonished them, "Search the Scriptures; for in them ye think ye have eternal life: and they are they which testify of me. For had ye believed Moses, ye would have believed me; for he wrote of me" (John 5:39, 46).

What would they have discovered had they heeded His counsel? They would have discovered that He was the King of kings who first came as the Suffering Servant. They would have seen Him as both the Sacrificial Lamb and the Lion of the Tribe of Judah. They would have realized that the One whom they constantly confronted and ultimately rejected was the very One who came to save them. They would have recognized Him as their Creator. They would have accepted Him as the Messiah whom they claim to look forward to.

Perhaps the most recognizable attribute of the God of the Bible is that of Creator. His servant Moses, without and theological presupposition nor intellectual philosophy, unequivocally revealed to us, "In the beginning God created the heaven and the earth" (Genesis 1:1). Some four thousand years later, John, one of the closest disciples of Jesus Christ, declared, "In the beginning was the Word, and the Word was with God, and the Word was God. The same was in the beginning with God. All things were made by him; and without him was not anything made that was made... And the Word was made flesh, and dwelt among us, and we beheld his glory, the glory as of the only begotten of the Father, full of grace and truth" (John 1:1-3, 14).

Paul, formerly called Saul, who was a persecutor of the early Christian church, ultimately came to that realization and exclaimed, "God, who at sundry times and in divers manners spake in time past unto the fathers by the prophets, hath in these last days spoken unto us by his Son, whom he hath appointed heir of all things, by whom also he made the worlds; Who being the brightness of his glory, and the express image of His person, and upholding all things by the word of his power, when He had by Himself purged our sins, sat down on the right hand of the Majesty on high" (Hebrews 1:1-3).

The overarching theme of the Bible is Jesus Christ. He is the central figure in both the Old and New Testaments. He was not only a prophet; but His own testimony and that of others give undeniable credibility to His life and ministry, proving that He is indeed God. There has been no other personality in human history whose life has been so precisely predicted and has so accurately came to pass as that of Jesus Christ. The prophesies and their remarkable fulfillment testify of the singular life experience of Jesus Christ. Also, they unquestionably establish the supernatural nature of the Bible, life's manual for both believers and unbelievers. Jesus' claims as to who He is, coupled with the testimonies of the Bible writers, both Old and New Testaments, are beyond the realm of possibility of any other person being who they claim Jesus to be, God with us. He unabashedly claimed that He is the Bread of life, the Light of the world and the only means of through which every human being can find that universally heartfelt desire--restoration to the image of God-- eternal life.

Undoubtedly, the most startling declaration of who Jesus truly is was made by the ancient seer Isaiah. He foretold of Jesus' miraculous appearance on planet earth and who He truly is more than six hundred years before His birth. Said the prophet, "Therefore the Lord himself shall give you a sign; Behold, a virgin shall conceive, and bear a son, and shall call his name Immanuel (Isaiah 7:14).

This prophecy was fulfilled with uncanny accuracy at the time appointed. The Gospel writer, Matthew, explains; "Now all this was done, that it might be fulfilled which was spoken of the Lord by the prophet, saying, Behold, a virgin shall be with child, and shall bring forth a son, and they shall call his name

Emmanuel, which being interpreted is, God with us" (Matthew 1:22-23).

All the other names and titles by which Yahweh was addressed in the Old Testament, Jesus claimed as His own or was referred to by the writers of the New Testament. This is a startling phenomenon that proves beyond the shadow of a doubt that the God of the Hebrew Scriptures is the Jesus of the Christian Church. Here is perhaps the most convincing example: "Thus saith the Lord the King of Israel, and his redeemer the Lord of hosts; I am the first, and I am the last; and beside me there is no God" (Isaiah 44:6). Then Jesus boldly proclaims, "I am Alpha and Omega, the beginning and the ending, which is, and which was, and which is to come, the Almighty" (Revelation 1:8).

Jesus being God is a concept beyond any human comprehension. The apostle Paul, with all of his Hebrew learning and Greek scholarship, coupled with his profound Christian experience, was forced to declare, "And without controversy great is the mystery of godliness: God was manifest in the flesh, justified in the Spirit, seen of angels, preached unto the Gentiles, believed on in the world, received up into glory" (1 Timothy 3:16).

The above by no means exhaust what the Scriptures testify of who Jesus truly is. However, they are more than sufficient to establish the fact that Jesus is verily God. As God's people we must, by faith, accept this crucial Bible truth and reject any other philosophy. Paul, quoting the ancient prophet Habakkuk, simply states, "For I am not ashamed of the gospel of Christ: for it is the power of God unto salvation to everyone that believeth; to the Jew first, and also to the Greek. For therein is the righteousness of God revealed from faith to faith: as it is written, the just shall live by faith" (Romans 1:16-17).

Jesus Christ cannot be reduced to the same level of Mohamed, Krishna, the Dali Lama, Confucius, the Pope or any other religious teacher. In fact, any so-called religious teacher who fails to uplift Jesus for who He truly is, God with us, must not be trusted and followed if eternal life is what you seek. Only God has eternal life, therefore He is the only One who can give it. The apostle John rightly states, "And this is life eternal, that they might know thee the only true God, and Jesus Christ, whom thou hast sent" (John 17:3).

Jesus Christ is verily God manifested in the flesh. None other human person can rightfully claim that office nor has the authority to assume that prerogative. He is indeed God with us, the Only Savior of the world. He alone has the power to overcome death and bless with eternal life. Only Jesus is endowed with that attribute. The Blessed Hope is exclusive to Him.

As we have looked at some of the prophecies that so clearly identify and reveal Jesus as God with us; let us focus forward and upward to the most glorious of them all--His soon return to take home the faithful to live eternally with Him as He had originally intended. As you have seen all of the other prophesies fulfilled, you can rest secured and assured of His last promise: "And this is the will of him that sent me, that everyone which seeth the Son, and believeth on him, may have everlasting life: and I will raise him up at the last day" (John 6:40).

Be faithful and one day you, like Paul and all the redeemed, will get opportunity to look into the mystery of how He can be the Son, separate from the Father; and the Son who is One with the Father at the same time. While you are delving into that, you will also have plenty of time to learn of how He is the Lion and also the Lamb. You can investigate how He is your Prophet, Priest and King at the same time. That's a glimpse of what eternity with Him would be like. For now, just accept Him for whom He and the prophets say that He is, God with us--the One who died for you.

Chapter 3

CONTEMPLATING CALVARY

E aster is the time of the year when we hear a lot about the cross of Calvary. But what does it really mean?

To some, it is a good luck charm to be worn around the neck. Yet others display it as evidence that they are Christians. It has become a decorative piece to adorn church edifices. To too many, the cross is an object to be worshipped. None of this, however, embodies what God intended this emblem of supreme sacrifice to be. The cross of Calvary was not designed to be taken lightly as so many take it to be. God never desired that the sacrifice of His Only Begotten Son should be reduced to any of the above or to an annual festival of display and revelry that cheapens the cost of our salvation.

The cross of Calvary is God's object lesson illustrating to the world the cost of sin and the price of redemption of sinners. It is here that justice and mercy meet each other. At Calvary, love and hate confronted each other and praise God, love won. The prophet Isaiah gives a clearer definition of Jesus' mission to ransom and reunite the human family back to Himself and our Father. He painfully counseled his nation back then and us today, "He is despised and rejected of men; a man of sorrows, and acquainted with grief: and we hid as it were our faces from him; he was despised, and we esteemed him not. Surely, he hath borne our griefs, and carried our sorrows: yet we did esteem him stricken, smitten of God, and afflicted. But he was wounded for our transgressions, he was bruised for our iniquities: the chastisement of our peace was upon him; and with his stripes we are healed" (Isaiah 53:3-5). This is the essence of Calvary. It was the down-payment for our ransom and reunion.

The apostle Paul illustrates it best. Says he, "For the wages of sin is death, but the Gift of God is eternal life through Christ Jesus" (Romans 6:23). The apostle John, with a sense of unexplainable curiosity, asks: "What manner of love the Father hath bestowed upon us that we should be called the sons of God" (1 John 3:1). Jesus Himself declared, "Greater love hath no man than this, that a man lay down His life for his friends" (John 15:13).

The Man of Calvary teaches us: "For God so loved the world, that He gave His only begotten son, that whosoever believeth on Him will not perish but have everlasting life...for God sent not His Son into the world to condemn the world, but that the world through Him might be saved" (John 3:16,17).

On Calvary, we witnessed the greatest demonstration of love that the world ever knew or will ever know. We beheld the supreme sacrifice of all eternity. The One who is infinite in power, Master of the universe, rich in principalities and planets gave it all up to become one with us sinners; so that we may one day become one with Him. The apostle Paul therefore declared, "For ye know the grace of our Lord Jesus Christ, that, though He was rich, yet for your sakes He became poor, that ye through His poverty might be rich" (2 Corinthians 8:9).

Our Lord and Savior, Jesus Christ, who knew now sin, became sin for us that we may become righteous in Him. He took upon Him our transgressions in which He had no part; so that we may obtain salvation which we do not deserve. Paul continues, "For He had made Him to be sin for us, who knew no sin: that we might be made the righteousness of God in Him" (2 Corinthians 5:21).

On Calvary, Jesus Christ subdued His power of divinity that He may suffer with humanity. This is a great mystery that our finite minds cannot comprehend. It is the enduring appeal of Calvary.

He was slain from the foundations of the world that we may live with Him throughout the ceaseless ages of eternity. He endured the pain and agony of an ignominious death on Calvary, in order that we may enjoy the bliss of eternal life. On Calvary, He cried so that we may rejoice. He became mortal that we may be made immortal. In the process, He traded His righteousness for our unrighteousness. He descended to earth that we may ascend to heaven. The nails that held Him to the cross were the keys that set us free from the prison house of sin. This is the true meaning of Calvary. Contemplate it today. The apostle Peter sums it up in this way, "Forasmuch as ye know that ye were not redeemed with corruptible things, as silver and gold, from your vain conversation received by tradition from your fathers; but with the precious blood of Christ, as of a lamb without blemish and without spot" (1 Peter 18-19).

The Jesus of Calvary, not the sun of Easter, is the One we should worship, every day of our lives. Through His suffering, He became victorious that we may yet have an Advocate with the Father. The apostle John counsels us, "My little children, these things write I unto you, that ye sin not. And if any man sin, we have an advocate with the Father, Jesus Christ the righteous" (1 John 2:1).

As you contemplate Calvary, don't neglect to meditate on His life before the cross. The apostle Peter reminds us: "For even hereunto were we called: because Christ also suffered for us, leaving us an example that we may follow His steps. Who did no sin, neither was guile found in his mouth: Who, when he was reviled, reviled not again; when he suffered, he threatened not; but committed himself to him that judgeth righteously" (1 Peter 2:21). His fellow apostle, Paul, agrees, "For if, when we were enemies, we were reconciled to God by the death of His Son, much more, being reconciled, we shall be saved by His life" (Romans 5:10). That's the true meaning of Calvary.

Too many tend to go only from the manger to the cross, woefully failing to grasp the fullness of Bethlehem and the pricelessness of Calvary. But, as you go from Christmas to Easter, do ever remember that He is no longer a babe in Bethlehem. We cannot neglect or belittle His sacrifice on Calvary; but He is no longer suffering on the cross either. He is our risen High Priest sitting on the right hand of His Father and our Father interceding for us. So the apostle Paul lovingly encourages us, "For we have not an High Priest which cannot be touched with the feeling of our infirmities; but was in all points tempted like as we are, yet without sin...Let us therefore come boldly to the throne of grace, that we may obtain mercy and find grace to help in a time of need" (Hebrews 4:15, 16). That too is because of Calvary. Contemplate it today.

The true meaning of Calvary is that we are all sinners and are in need of the Savior. That Savior, the Only Savior, Jesus Christ, came and lived a perfect life as an example for us to follow in His footsteps. He took our place on Calvary's hill, conquered death, that we may find our way back to God and have eternal life (John 3:16). That's the truth about Calvary.

What is your trial today? Whatever you may be going through, contemplate Calvary. But don't stop there. Follow the slain Lamb as He becomes your risen Savior and faithful High Priest, pleading on your behalf with His Father and your Father. Get ready for Him as He shall soon burst the clouds of heaven and come to take His faithful ones to spend the ceaseless ages of eternity with Him. He has not made the down payment at Calvary to not return and consummate the contract. We are reminded by the apostle Paul, "For the Lord himself shall descend from heaven with a shout, with the voice of the archangel, and with the trump of God: and the dead in Christ shall rise first: Then we which are alive and remain shall be caught up together with them in the clouds, to meet the Lord in the air: and so shall we ever be with the Lord. Wherefore comfort one another with these words" (1 Thessalonians 4:16-18).

Whatever your temptation, whatever your challenge, your Savior has been there. As He has overcome, so with Him, you can also overcome. Ellen G. White, the renowned nineteenth century Bible commentator, tells us in her book, Desire of Ages, a classic on the life of Christ: "By His humanity, Christ touched humanity; by His divinity, He lays hold upon the throne of God. As the Son of man, He gave us an example of obedience; as the Son of God, He gives us power to obey" (Desire of Ages, pg. 23, E.G. White.) So Paul assures us, " There hath no temptation taken you but such as is common to man; but God is faithful, who will not suffer you to be tempted above that you are able; but with the temptation also make a way to escape, that ye may be able to bear" (1 Corinthians 10:13). That way of escape is through Calvary. Contemplate it today.

Contemplate it, not simply as a time of revelry, Easter baskets, painted eggs or bunny rabbits, nor a time of worshiping the sun of Easter; but contemplate Calvary as the supreme sacrifice and great mystery that tempers the passions, fortifies the mind, refines the taste and ennobles the character. Contemplate it as the means to equip you for service here below and prepare you for residency in the mansions He has gone to prepare for you in the heavens above. Contemplate it as God's unfathomable love for us sinners. Contemplate Calvary as the only means that gives peace beyond understanding. There is no problem you are facing that Calvary cannot solve. Contemplate it today. Upon it was nailed the One who died for you.

Chapter 4

THE SLAIN LAMB

*I*t was on a Friday afternoon at 3:00 PM almost two thousand years ago. The Jewish High Priest was about to offer the evening sacrifice on behalf of the nation of Israel. It was a tradition they practiced for more than two thousand years...a ceremony that goes back to the beginning of time in the Garden of Eden (Genesis 3:21). But this sacrifice was different. For as the priest raised his hand with the knife that was to slay the innocent lamb, the heavens shudder, the sky became dark, the earth quaked violently, and the veil of the temple was rent from top to bottom as by an unseen hand.

The apostle Matthew recounted that fearful and memorable event thus, "And, behold, the veil of the temple was rent in twain from the top to the bottom; and the earth did quake, and the rocks rent; and the graves were opened; and many bodies of the saints which slept arose" (Matthew 27:51-52).

The apostle Paul, in trying to explain this phenomenon to his countrymen, declared, "So Christ was once offered to bear the sins of many; and unto them that look for him shall he appear the second time without sin unto salvation" (Hebrews 9:28). In fact, Paul wanted his countrymen to know that those animals they sacrificed and the rituals they so faithfully practiced for thousands of years, were figures and types of this reality. Jesus Christ fulfilled them to the letter on that fateful Friday evening.

When Adam and Eve first sinned and their communion with God was broken in Eden, He [God] explained to them the great controversy they had entered upon and the devastating effect it would have on their lives. He then introduced to them His plan for their ransom from the consequences of their disobedience and reunion to close communion with Him. It was a plan that was conceived in the heavenly sanctuary long before the first humans were created, and later separated from their loving Creator by that baleful thing called sin.

John, the Revelator, in foretelling of the great end-time apostasy and persecution of God's people, points us back and reminds us of the supreme sacrifice that was made for our salvation. He declares, "And all that dwell upon the earth shall worship him, whose names are not written in the book of life of the Lamb slain from the foundation of the world" (Revelation 13:8). John, as he gazed down through the ages saw the entire world following the antichrist power of Bible prophecy. But he is careful to remind God's people that the same provision that was made for our first parents, Adam and Eve, will be available to them in the closing scenes of earth's history. That provision, that remedy is the Slain Lamb-- our Lord and Savior, Jesus Christ.

In the beginning, God unveiled to Adam and Eve His plan to restore their broken relationship with Him. In the process of time, He unveiled more details about that plan as he commanded his servant, Moses, "And let them make Me a sanctuary; that I may dwell among them. According to all that I shew thee, after the pattern of the tabernacle, and the pattern of all the instruments thereof, even so shall ye make it" (Exodus 25:8-9). Because of His abundant love and matchless mercy, God wanted his people to come to know Him and thus reignite that personal relationship with them which they had lost in Eden. Ultimately, that's what the sanctuary and its services are all about, a saving relationship with our Creator and Redeemer, Jesus Christ.

As we examine the ancient Israeli sanctuary and its Feast Days, we will discover that they were that plan, in type, that pointed to our Lord and Savior, Jesus Christ, the timeline and His work for our salvation.

Before we get to the Feast Days, let's look at the basic, fundamental function of the earthly sanctuary that God instructed Moses to build. It was God's way of telling His people that He wanted them to know Him, His work on their behalf and His profound desire to have a saving relationship with them. Every component, from the largest curtain to the tiniest piece of furniture of that sanctuary, or tabernacle as it is sometimes called, represented some aspect of the plan of salvation and the life and ministry of Jesus Christ.

For example, the shewbread that was provided every Sabbath morning was a symbol of Jesus Christ, who would declare, "I am the living bread which came down from heaven: if any man eat of this bread, he shall lice forever: and the bread that I will give is my flesh, which I will give for the life of the world' (John 6:51). He also declared, "I am the light of the world: he that followeth Me shall not walk in darkness, but shall have the light of life" (John 8:12). Indeed, the seven-branch candlestick in the Holy Place of the ancient Israeli sanctuary typified the Messiah who would come to shed His light of truth throughout the earth. The incense that was burned, on altar of payer in the same compartment of the earthy sanctuary, represented the righteousness of Jesus without which no one can be saved.

Ultimately, the sanctuary and its services were designed to help the children of Israel, and us today, see, experience, and comprehend the workings of Jesus Christ in the heavenly sanctuary on our behalf in a very practical way. The psalmist Asaph sums it up this way, "Thy way, O God, is in the sanctuary: who is so great a God as our God?" (Ps 77:13). Here Asaph is simply referring to the manner in which God operates with regard to our salvation from sin, ransom from its penalty, which is death, and eternal reunion with Him.

Following God's specific instructions, Moses oversaw the construction of the most magnificent and beautiful structure of his time. It was pitched in the wilderness and travelled with the Israelites throughout their 40+ years of wilderness journey from Sinai to Canaan. Around it was the courtyard enclosed by linen curtains and suspended with silver hooks on brass pillars. The structure itself was 45ft x 15ft and located on the western side of the courtyard which was 150ft x 75ft. It contained two compartments, the Holy Place and the Most Holy Place.

The ancient Israeli sanctuary and its services were an object lesson of God's love, His justice and His mercy. As the people performed the rituals and followed the instructions of the priests, they got a better understanding of who God is and what He required of their lives. As a result, they were shielded from the false concepts of worship that surrounded them, except of course, when they chose to go contrary to God's will as revealed in the sanctuary.

The knowledge of the sanctuary and the lessons it teaches have been largely neglected and forgotten by most of Christendom. In the process, they have deprived themselves of the power the sanctuary offers to live a victorious Christian life. As a direct consequence, they have allowed themselves to be engrossed in and are deceived into accepting a plethora of false doctrines, firmly believing them to be true. In an age when knowledge is increased beyond measure in the secular world, God's professed people are subscribing to an unending array of false Biblical teachings and vain, perverted theologies. It is for this reason that a prayerful study of the sanctuary is vitally important to those who call themselves Christians.

The sanctuary gives the only correct view of God and His dealings with His people. It reveals God's true perspective of sin and His plan for human redemption from it. In the sanctuary, all false doctrines are turned upside down and God's truth comes alive in their right places with clarity, brightness and glory.

The apostle Paul, in attempting to persuade his fellow Hebrew brethren that Jesus Christ was the promised Messiah, declared, "Now of the things which we have spoken this is the sum: We have such an high priest, who is set on the right hand of the throne of the Majesty in the heavens; A minister of the sanctuary, and of the true tabernacle, which the Lord pitched, and not man. For every high priest is ordained to offer gifts and sacrifices: wherefore it is of necessity that this man (Jesus Christ) have somewhat also to offer" (Hebrews 8:1-3). And if Jesus has something to offer then we want to direct our focus to where He is--in the heavenly sanctuary. Thus Paul declared, "For we have not an High Priest which cannot be touched with the feelings with our infirmities; but was in all points tempted like as we are, yet without sin let us therefore come boldly to the throne of grace, that we may obtain mercy, and find grace to help in a time of need" (Hebrews 4:15-16).

M.L. Andreasen, a noted scholar on the subject, writes: "There are professed Christians who do not see much of importance or value in the God-ordained temple services; yet the gospel plan of salvation as revealed in the New Testament is made clearer by an understanding of the Old Testament. In fact, it may confidently be said that he who understands the Levitical system of the Old Testament can much better understand and appreciate the New Testament. The one foreshadows the other and is a type of it" (The Sanctuary Service, pg. 20, M.L. Andreasen).

Perhaps the most important reason to study and understand the Sanctuary is because Our Savior admonishes us to study the Jewish Scriptures (Old Testament) to find out who He truly is. (Luke 25:27; John 5:39; 2 Timothy 3:15-17). Jesus was verily speaking of the revelation of Himself in the ancient sanctuary and its services. The Feast Days, in particular, outlines and gives a clear timeline of His work and mission as our Sacrifice, Savior, High Priest and soon–coming King.

When prayerfully studied and understood, the sanctuary will shelter us from the strong, overwhelming delusions that are rapidly spreading in intensity and scope around the world, particularly in professed Christendom. It is only by knowing Jesus Christ and understanding His work in His sanctuary that we can be shielded from the delusions of the enemy and be protected from what is to shortly come upon the world as an overwhelming surprise.

The psalmist David declares, "They have seen thy goings of my God, my King, in the sanctuary" (Psalm 68:24). So, therefore, the apostle Paul could confidently declare, "For unto us was the gospel preached, as well as unto them: but the word preached did not profit them, not being mixed with faith in them that heard it" (Hebrews 3:16).

Here now are explanations of those Feasts Days and their fulfillment in the life and ministry of Jesus Christ, the Slain Lamb.

Passover/Unleavened Bread

"The fourteenth day of the first month at even is the Lord's Passover...and on the fifteenth day of the same month is the feast of unleavened bread unto the Lord" (Leviticus 23:5-6). For I will pass through the land of Egypt this night and will smite all the firstborn in the land of Egypt, both man and beast; and against all the gods of Egypt I will execute judgment: I am the Lord. And the blood shall be to you for a token upon the houses where ye are: and when I see the blood, I will pass over you, and the plague shall not be upon you to destroy you, when I smite the land of Egypt. (Exodus 12:12, 13)

Fulfillment in Jesus Christ

Only those who have accepted Jesus Christ as their Lord and Savior from sin, covered with His blood and obey His commandments will be shielded from the wrath of God when the last seven plagues are poured out upon planet earth. So His servant Paul appeals to us, "Purge out therefore the old leaven that ye may be a new lump as ye are unleavened. For even Christ our Passover is sacrificed for us" (I Corinthians 5:7) (Matthew 27:51-53).

First Fruits

"Speak unto the children of Israel, and say unto them, when ye come into the land which I give unto you, ye shall reap the harvest thereof, then ye shall bring a sheaf of the first fruits of your harvest unto the priest... and ye shall wave the sheaf before the Lord to be accepted for you" (Leviticus 23:10-11).

Fulfillment in Jesus Christ

"But now is Christ risen from the dead, and become the first fruit of them that slept... But every man in his own order: Christ the first fruits; afterward they that are Christ at his coming" (1 Corinthians 15:20).

Pentecost

"And ye shall count unto you from the morrow after the Sabbath from the day that ye brought the sheaf of the wave offering; seven Sabbaths shall be complete: Even unto the morrow after the seventh Sabbath shall ye number fifty days; and ye shall offer a new meat offering unto the Lord" (Leviticus 23:15, 16)

Fulfillment in Jesus Christ

The Day of Pentecost was a time of jubilation for the ancient Israelites, celebrating their deliverance from Egyptian bondage. "And when the day of Pentecost were fully come, they were all with one accord in one place... and suddenly there came a sound from heaven as a mighty rushing wind, and it filled the house where they were sitting... and they were filled with the Holy Ghost, and began to speak with other tongues, as the Spirit gave them utterance" (Acts 1:1, 2, 4).

The gift of the Holy Ghost was poured out upon the disciples by Jesus Christ on the fiftieth day following his crucifixion. As Jesus was anointed as our High Priest in the Heavenly Sanctuary, the Holy Spirit descended upon the disciples in Jerusalem on the Day of Pentecost.

Luke 23:54-56; 24:1,13	3 Day	Death, burial and resurrection.
Acts 1:3	40 Days	Life on earth after resurrection.
Exodus 29:7, 35	7 Days	Anointing as High Priest in heavenly sanctuary.
Total	**50 Days**	**Pentecost**

Trumpets /Atonement

"Speak unto the children of Israel, saying, in the seventh month, in the feast day of the month, shall ye have a Sabbath, a memorial of blowing trumpets in holy convocation... Also on the tenth day of this seventh month, there shall be a day of atonement: it shall be a holy convocation unto you; and ye shall afflict your souls and offer an offering made by fire unto the Lord" (Leviticus 23:24, 27).

Fulfillment in Jesus Christ

"And I saw another angel fly in the midst of heaven, having the everlasting gospel to preach unto them that dwell upon the earth, and to every nation, and kindred, and tongue and people... saying with a loud voice, "fear God and give glory to Him; for the hour of His judgment is come: and worship Him that made the heaven and earth, and the sea, and the fountain of waters" (Revelation 14: 6-7). "He that is unjust, let him be unjust still: and he which is filthy, let him be filthy still; and he that is righteous, let him be righteous still: and he that is holy, let him be holy still...And behold, I come quickly; and my reward is with Me, to give every man according to his work shall be" (Revelation 22:11-12).

NOTE: The call to come back to the worship of the true God, the God of creation, the God of the Sabbath, goes out to all humanity today. That was indeed the purpose of the ancient Feast of Trumpets which was immediately followed by the Day Atonement, a time of judgement, verily, the times in which we live.

Tabernacles/Booths

"Speak unto the children of Israel, saying, the fifteenth day of this seventh month shall be the Feast of

Tabernacles (Ingathering) for seven days unto the Lord... Also in the fifteenth day of the seventh month, when ye have gathered in the fruit of the land, ye shall keep a feast unto the Lord seven days: on the first day shall be a Sabbath and on the eight day shall be a Sabbath... Ye shall dwell in the booths seven days, all that are Israelite born shall dwell in booths" (Leviticus 23:39, 42).

Fulfillment in Jesus Christ

"Immediately after the tribulation of those days shall the sun be darkened, and the moon shall not give her light, and the stars shall fall from heaven, and the powers of the heavens shall be shaken: And then shall appear the sign of the Son of man in heaven: and then shall all the tribes of the earth mourn, and they shall see the Son of man coming in the clouds of heaven with power and great glory. And he shall send his angels with a great sound of a trumpet, and they shall gather together his elect from the four winds, from one end of heaven to the other...And I saw thrones, and they that sat upon them, and Judgment was given unto them. And I saw the souls of them which were beheaded for the witness of Jesus, and for the word of God, and which had not worshipped the beast, neither his image, neither had received the mark upon their foreheads, or in their hands; and they lived and reigned with Christ a thousand years" (Matthew 24:29-31) (Revelation 20:4) (Revelation 21:1-4).

NOTE: The feast of Tabernacles/Booths foreshadowed the return of Jesus Christ to earth to gather His elect and to take them to heaven for 1000 years. As the Jews returned to their homes after the feast, having dwelt in tabernacles and booths for seven days, so will the people of God return to an earth made new, after the thousand years, to spend the ceaseless ages of eternity with Him. He promises, "Blessed are the meek: for they shall inherit the earth" (Matthew 5:5).

The Feasts Days provide an unbroken chain of divine truth regarding the life and ministry of Jesus Christ that cannot be found anyplace else. Central to Feast Days was the Slain Lamb, Jesus Christ our Savior and Lord—the One who died for you.

Chapter 5

WHY HE CAME

*P*erhaps the most quoted and best-known Scripture in the Bible is John 3:16-17. It reads, "For God so loved the world that He gave His only begotten Son, that whosoever believeth in Him should not perish but have everlasting life...For God sent not His son into the world to condemn the world; but that the world through Him might be saved."

But saved from what? The gospel writer Matthew answered assuredly, "And she shall bring forth a son, and thou shall call His name Jesus: for He shall save His people from their sins" (Matthew 1:21). These words were announced to Joseph, the espoused husband of Mary, by the angel Gabriel.

When God created man, His (God) purpose was that we would live with Him eternally. Unfortunately, man disobeyed God and the curse of sin, which is death, entered the picture. But an infinite, loving, omniscient God had a plan prepared by which man will be reconciled to and live eternally with Him as He originally intended. John writes in the book of Revelation about those who will be saved and restored to eternal life with God, their Creator: "And God shall wipe away all tears from their eyes; and there shall be no more death, neither sorrow, nor crying, neither shall there be any more pain: for the former things are passed away. (Revelation 21:8).

As John the Baptist, the forerunner of Jesus Christ, was preaching and baptizing on the river Jordon, he saw someone amid the crowd who particularly caught his attention. Dressed in the attire of the common people-- farmers, peasants, fishermen, and laborers who came to listen to John, this person had a distinctive state of being. His presence was simply awe-inspiring. Though dressed like the common folk, His gait was that of royalty. Impressed by the Holy Spirit, John was led to declare, "Behold the Lamb of God which taketh away the sin of the world" (John 1:29). The angel likewise announced to the shepherds as they watched over their flocks by night, "Fear not: for, behold, I bring you good tidings of great joy, which shall be to all people...for unto you is born in the city of David a Savior which is Christ the Lord" (Luke 2:10-11).

The reason that Jesus came is to save us from the penalty of sin, which is death. Sin separates us from God. The Gospel prophet Isaiah, informs us, "But your iniquities have separated between you and your God, and your sins have hid his face from you, that he will not hear" (Isaiah 59:2). But how does Jesus Christ reconcile us to His and our Father? First of all, He does it by giving us the Divine pattern which we should follow. The apostle Peter recorded, "For even hereunto were ye called: because Christ also suffered for us, leaving us an example, that ye should follow his steps: Who did no sin, neither was guile found in his mouth: Who, when he was reviled, reviled not again; when he suffered, he threatened not; but committed himself to him that judgeth righteously" (1Peter 2:21-23).

By Jesus' perfect, sinless life, God intends that we, by His grace, would be transformed into His image--the image in which He originally made us and from which we have fallen. So the apostle Paul admonishes us, "But we all with open face beholding as in a glass, the glory of the Lord are changed into the same image, from glory to glory even as by the Spirit of the Lord" (2 Corinthians 3:18). He continues, "For God who commanded the light to shine out of darkness, hath shined in our hearts, to give the knowledge of the glory of God in the face of Jesus Christ" (2 Corinthians 4:6).

Secondly, Jesus saves us by taking our place on Calvary's cross to die in our place. He did no sin and therefore did not deserve death. But because He loves us so much, He took upon Himself the penalty which we deserved. By so doing, He gives us the opportunity to live with Him eternally. The apostle Paul again reminds us, "But God commandeth His love towards us, in that, while we were yet sinners, Christ died for us...For if, when we were enemies, we were reconciled to God by the death of His son, much more, being reconciled we shall be saved by His life" (Romans 5:8, 10). The apostle continues, "To wit, that God was in Christ reconciling the world unto Himself, not imputing their trespasses unto them; and have committed unto us the word reconciliation" (2 Corinthians 5:19).

Further, Jesus ministers on our behalf in the Heavenly Sanctuary. The record reveals, "For we have not an High Priest which cannot be touched with the feeling of our infirmities, but was in all points tempted like as we are, yet without sin...Let us therefore come boldly unto the throne of grace, that we may obtain mercy and find grace to help in a time of need" (Hebrews 4:15-16).

Paul also tells us the time of His birth. Says he to saints at Galatia, "But when the fullness of time was come, God sent forth His Son born of a woman, made under the law...to redeem them that were under the law, that we might receive the adoption of sons" (Galatians 4: 4-5). Nothing more specific has been given to us about the time of the Savior's birth. Any other pronouncement is but vain tradition and intellectual speculation. But the world celebrates His birthday on December 25th. There is quite a lot of merriment, gift-sharing, singing and other accompaniments that have nothing to do with why He came. Nevertheless, many get the opportunity to hear about Him, somewhat; for what man intended for evil, a celebration of the sun god, the God of Creation turns into good. However, the reason for which He truly came is largely forgotten in the process. But how can this be?

And why the celebration on December 25th with the accompanying festivities? Some historical evidence gives us clues. Walter Woodburn Hyde, a reputed church historian writes, "Remains of the struggle between the religion of Christianity and the religion of Mithraism are found in two institutions adopted from its rival by Christianity in the fourth century. The two Mithraic days: December 25th, Dies Natalis Solis (birthday of the sun) as the birthday of Jesus; and Sunday, the venerable day of the sun, as Constantine called it in his edict of 321 AD" (Paganism to Christianity in the Roman Empire, pg., 60, Walter Woodburn Hyde).

This date, December 25th, and the honor given to it, by most Christians, has no Scriptural basis or Divine approval. It is a tradition of man, adopted by the church of the middle ages and handed down the world. Often we hear the assertion, "we know that December 25th is not the birthday of Jesus Christ, but". Whatever comes after the 'but', except for someone to take the opportunity to share the love and truth of Jesus, is largely immaterial. The apostle James warns us, "Therefore, to him that knoweth to do good and doeth it not, to him it is sin" (James 4:17). Our Lord and Savior, the very one who is supposedly celebrated on December 25th, declares, "This people honoureth Me with their lips, but their heart is far from Me...Howbeit, in vain do they worship

Me, teaching for doctrines the commandments of men" (Mark 7:6-7).

We cannot take that which God has condemned, and convert it to what He requires. Under whatever pretext we concoct, it is dangerous to know what God says and willfully chooses to do otherwise. The honoring of December 25th, as the birthday of our Blessed Savior, along with Sunday sacredness, stand out as the two greatest acts of rebellion against God in Christendom today.

The Christianized name for the pagan tradition honoring the sun is of course Christmas. "Christmas" is a contraction of the term "Christ's Mass". The word itself is an oxymoron, a contradiction in terms. Christ is the Light of the world. He is truth and He is life. The 'Mass' is a Papal ritual performed by its priests who claim in the process to bring down Christ from heaven and crucify Him afresh every time the Mass is celebrated. But Jesus Christ was sacrificed once. Paul, the learned apostle, teaches: "But this man, after he had offered one sacrifice for sins forever, sat down on the right hand of God" (Hebrews 10:12).

The Scripture does not tell us of the day Jesus was born nor does God asks us to celebrate a day in honor of His birth. There is no record of the decorating of the evergreen tree, the use of mistletoe, exchanging of gifts one to the other or Santa Claus. None of this can lead us to salvation, the only purpose for which Jesus came.

These popular practices are all adopted from pagan religions of old and passed on to God's people by the Roman Catholic Church.

The beloved apostle John speaks of the wide influence of the European Ecclesiastical Establishment: "And there came one of the seven angels which had the seven vials, and talked with me, saying unto me, Come hither; I will shew unto thee the judgment of the great whore that sitteth upon many waters: With whom the kings of the earth have committed fornication, and the inhabitants of the earth have been made drunk with the wine of her fornication" (Revelation 17:1-2). Christmas is certainly one of her strongest wines. The whole world has indeed been made drunk by it. By her association with the nations of the world, December 25th has become one of the most commercially profitable enterprises known to man. The church and the nations, ostensibly in the name of Christ, look forward to this time, not with a need for a Savior, but rather with a yearning for financial or other personal gain.

Thousands of years before the first advent of Jesus Christ, the pagan cultures of antiquity venerated December 25th and worshipped the mother/son icon which is now perceived as Mary holding her son, Jesus. This is a most powerful and deeply emotional phenomenon. Have you ever stopped to think that though Jesus was born about two thousand years ago, He never grows up, but continues to be a babe in His mother's arms? This imagery has nothing to do with our

Savior's birth and everything to do with the ancient cultic practice of mother/son worship. It permeates every pagan religion. In Egypt is was Isis with her son Horus. The Chinese venerate this image as Shing Moo and her son. To the Hindus, the icon is represented as Divaki, the mother and Krishna, the son.

How can so many go out and spend money that they do not have, placing themselves in debt, and all the while believing that they are honoring God? In what way do men and women praise God by engaging in drunkenness and gluttony? How can you uplift the name of Jesus by partying and engaging in illicit sexual activity? But you say that He is the reason for the season. Where is He in all of this?

At best, Christmas has become popular culture. To mix it with the birth of Jesus Christ does not make it Christian. Neither Christ, the apostles nor the early church endorsed such a practice. Popular culture, innocent and fun-filled as it may seem, can't save us. Only Jesus Christ can. But what should the Christian do in such an atmosphere? Someone suggested that we put Christ back in Christmas. Well, He was never there to begin with. What we can do is to do what we should be doing throughout the year, *i.e.* loving, caring, giving and telling others about Him, particularly His soon coming; not as a babe in a manger, but as Lord of lords and King of kings. We do not need a pagan festival to do this. Yes indeed, Christmas draws some attention to the name of

Christ. But Christ declares, "And I, if I be lifted up from the earth will draw all men unto me" (John 12:32).

When Christians live like Christ intended them to, with or without Christmas, all men will know that there is a Savior whose name is Jesus Christ. As we study His word, pray and follow His example in serving humanity, then the world will know that a Savior was born. We don't need pagan accompaniments to do this. Christ stands alone, apart from the traditions of men and the practices of the world. So should we.

Finally, the birth of Christ has nothing to with a celebration on December 25th; but all to do with the transformation of our characters to be like Him, so that we may go home with Him when He comes…very soon. The apostle Paul admonishes us, "And be not confirmed to this world, but be ye transformed by the renewing of your mind, that ye may prove what is that good, and acceptable, and perfect, will of God" (Romans 12:2).

One of America's most influential religious leaders eloquently portrayed why He came, "Satan was exulting that he had succeeded in debasing the image of God in humanity. Then Jesus came to restore in man the image of his Maker. None but Christ can fashion anew the character that has been ruined by sin. He came to expel the demons that had controlled the will. He came to lift us up from the dust, to reshape the marred character after the pattern of His divine character, and to make it beautiful with His own glory (Desire of Ages, pg. 37, E.G. White,).

For this reason only, He came. He is the One who died for you.

Chapter 6

THE REST OF THE STORY

*D*espite the many distractions from the true purpose for which the birth of Christ is supposed to be celebrated, the season provides a great opportunity to shine for God. At that time of the year, people tend to be more receptive to spiritual things. Not that they are particularly more spiritual; but rather, simply because of the name of Jesus is mentioned and the world-wide celebration of His birth, hearts are open to spiritual things. People are so much nicer and kinder. They are in the spirit of gift-giving and receiving. If you offer them the gift of a Truth-filled book, they will gladly accept it.

This is not a time to debate the merits of whether Jesus was born on December 25th, nor to confront others on the pagan origins of the day. Instead, it is best to take full advantage of the opportunity to let men and women know of His love for them, of their need to give their lives to Him and to accept Him as their Lord and Savior from sin. The yearly festival of sun worship, pretending it to be the celebration of the birth of the world's Redeemer, is indeed an opportune time in which to lift up Jesus as the Only Savior of all humanity. He admonishes us, "And I, if I be lifted up from the earth, will draw all men unto Me" (John 12:32). The season provides so much opportunity for men and women to come to know Jesus. Whatever each of us may do at this season is a matter of conscience between us and our God. I simply would like to share the rest of the story with you.

The apostle Paul teaches that whosoever preaches the Gospel, in whatever manner, and for whatever reason it is preached, it is profitable and we should rejoice. He writes, "Some indeed preach Christ even of envy and strife; and some also of good will: The one preach Christ of contention, not sincerely, supposing to add affliction to my bonds: But the other of love, knowing that I am set for the defense of the gospel. What then? Notwithstanding, every way, whether in pretense, or in truth, Christ is preached; and I therein do rejoice, yea, and will rejoice" (Philippians 1:15-18). We should rejoice with Paul and with the whole world that the Savior was born, who is Christ the Lord. Even those who do not call themselves Christians rejoice and celebrate His birth. No one can escape the sentiment of the season as the name of Jesus is lifted up at Christmastime.

I thank God for His birth. I thank God that He is no longer a babe in a manger gripped in His mother's arms. I rejoice in the fact that the Babe of Bethlehem is God's supreme gift to the human family. I rejoice that He grew up to live a sinless life and left it as an example for us to follow His steps. I praise God that He paid the ultimate price--His life as a ransom for my sins and yours that we may have a right back to the tree of life. I am excited that He has given me the blessed hope of eternal life in His resurrection from the tomb on the third day. I praise God for Him being my heavenly High Priest that I can come to Him with my joys, sorrows, and petitions. I look forward with joyous anticipation to His soon return as Lord of Lords and King of kings.

The Bible gives us the only accurate account of the origins and history of humanity. It teaches us that our Creator gave us our perfect, wonderful world with all its unspeakable beauty which He created by His word out of nothingness. Then, He created our first parents in His own image. Finally, He gave us His Sabbath rest as a reminder to us of who He truly is: theirs and our Creator. Therefore, we can depend on Him for everything we need. But something most tragic happened. The Bible says that our first parents disobeyed God's command. This is called sin and it separates us from our Creator. The apostle John writes: "Whosoever committeth sin transgresseth also the law: for sin is the transgression of the law" (1 John 3:4). The apostle Paul gives us the remedy: "For the wages of sin is death; but the gift of God is eternal life through Jesus Christ our Lord" (Romans 6:23).

So, some four thousand years after that fateful day in Eden when sin entered the picture, the Gift, the solution for the sin problem, was presented. The apostle

Matthew records, "Now when Jesus was born in Bethlehem of Judaea in the days of Herod the king, behold, there came wise men from the east to Jerusalem, Saying, Where is He that is born King of the Jews? For we have seen His star in the east and are come to worship Him" (Matthew 2:1-2).

But, who were these wise men from the east? Most scholars agree that they had come from Babylon. This magnificent nation was perhaps the greatest empire of the ancient world. It was a place of wealth, knowledge, and magnificence. The empire is legendary for its splendor and beauty. It had a highly developed culture. Its scholars were well versed in Science, Mathematics, Philosophy, Astronomy, Art, Architecture and all the other known disciplines of the human experience. The wise men were also learned in the Hebrew Scriptures, having studied them from God's people who were captives in their land for more than seventy years. They discovered from those Scriptures that: "There shall come a Star out of Jacob, and a Scepter shall rise out of Israel" (Numbers 24:17).

On that memorable night almost two thousand years ago, the wise men of Babylon, having studied both the Hebrew Scriptures and the movements of the heavenly bodies, observed what they believed to be that star that would lead to the promised Messiah. They followed the star to the Babe in Bethlehem. Not only did they find Him; but Matthew records that they brought precious gifts to honor Him. He writes, "And when they were come into the house, they saw the young child with Mary his mother, and fell down, and worshipped him: and when they had opened their treasures, they presented unto him gifts; gold, and frankincense and myrrh" (Matthew 2:11).

The gifts of the wise men from the east were not randomly selected gifts. God does not do anything in an arbitrary fashion. It was the God of all creation that inspired them to bring those specific gifts to the Babe of Bethlehem. These gifts were prophesies of who the receiver was. They foretold of what He would do on our behalf to ransom humanity from this world of sin and woe and reunite us back to our Creator God. In these gifts we find the rest of the story. They were figures of God's Plan of Redemption for our wretched souls. The entire Plan of Salvation was wrapped in the gold, the frankincense, and the myrrh.

Let us, first take a look at the myrrh. In the book of John, chapter 3, the Bible tells us that a very respectable, important, and highly revered Jewish leader came to Jesus, in secrecy, in the darkness of the night. He engaged Jesus in a conversation about salvation. That man, Nicodemus, was stunned and astonished at Jesus' simple presentation of the doctrine of salvation. Jesus' revelation defied Nicodemus' scholarly acumen, uprooted his theological moorings and challenged his philosophical presuppositions. The Divine Teacher's simple answer must have bewildered Nicodemus for not only its simplicity; but also for its profound impact upon his mind. Jesus told Nicodemus and is telling us today that in order to enter God's kingdom, we must be born again (John 3:1-21). He related to Nicodemus and to His people today that the old carnal man must die and we must be born again of His Holy Spirit.

At first, Nicodemus did not understand what Jesus meant. But 3½ years later, Nicodemus fully understands God's Plan of Salvation and embraces the Lamb which John declared 'would take away the sin of the world'. So now, Nicodemus comes openly, revealing to us the meaning of the myrrh that the wise men brought from the east. John records: "And there came also Nicodemus, which at the first came to Jesus by night, and brought a mixture of MYRRH and aloes, about a hundred-pound weight. Then took they the body of Jesus, and wound it in linen clothes with the spices, as the manner of the Jews is to bury" (John 19:39-40). Paul tells us, "But God commendeth his love toward us, in that, while we were yet sinners, Christ died for us" (Romans 5:8). The myrrh of the wise men of the east represented Jesus' sacrifice--the price that He would pay for our sins so that we can be reunited with Him. The wise men of the east were prophesying of this glorious event in the gift of myrrh to the Babe of Bethlehem. They were pointing to the cross of Calvary where the battered, blood-stained body of the babe would be nailed for our salvation. The myrrh prophesied of the balm that Jesus' sacrifice provides for the sinner.

WHO IS THIS JESUS WHO DIED FOR YOU?

Now let's look at the frankincense. The apostle Paul, in trying to help his Hebrew brethren truly understand the meaning of the ancient Jewish sanctuary and sacrificial system, writes to them in the book of Hebrews. Having given them a thorough explanation of the symbols and types of the earthly sanctuary, the center piece of their economy, he then concludes, "Now of the things which we have spoken this is the sum: We have such an high priest, who is set on the right hand of the throne of the Majesty in the heavens; a minister of the sanctuary, and of the true tabernacle, which the Lord pitched, and not man" (Hebrews 8:1-2).

In that ancient system of rites and rituals, which the apostle Paul addresses in the book of Hebrews, frankincense was the main ingredient with which other spices were mixed to form the incense that the High Priest used in the daily services. And what did he use it for? Moses tells us in the book of Exodus, the 30th chapter, beginning at verse 7. He writes, "And Aaron shall burn thereon sweet incense every morning" And what was that incense made of? Moses continues: "And the Lord said unto Moses, Take unto thee sweet spices, stacte, and onycha, and galbanum; these sweet spices with pure FRANKINCENSE: of each shall there be a like weight" (Exodus 30:34). Frankincense was also used to anoint the seven-branch golden candle stick, the meat offerings, and the table of shewbread in the first apartment of the sanctuary, commonly called the Holy Place. (Leviticus 2:1-2, 24:7). John the Revelator, in prophetic vision, tells us what he saw in the heavenly sanctuary which is the reality that was represented by the earthly tabernacle in ancient Israel. He records, "And another angel came and stood at the altar, having a golden censer; and there was given unto him much incense, that he should offer it with the prayers of all saints upon the golden altar which was before the throne" (Revelation 8:3).

So, what does the frankincense represent? It represents the merits and righteousness of Jesus Christ as our heavenly High Priest, not only to hear, but to answer our prayers. For it is only as our prayers are mixed with Jesus' righteousness that they can be accepted of the Father. The incense, with frankincense as its main ingredient, represents the work of Jesus Christ as He intercedes on our behalf in the work of sanctification that we may be ready to go home with Him when He comes. The apostle Paul encourages and consoles us: "Seeing then that we have a great High Priest, that is passed into the heavens, Jesus the Son of God, let us hold fast our profession. For we have not an high priest which cannot be touched with the feeling of our infirmities; but was in all points tempted like as we are, yet without sin. Let us therefore come boldly unto the throne of grace, that we may obtain mercy, and find grace to help in time of need" (Hebrews 4:14-16).

Our prayers, our witnessing, our study of His Holy word-the Bible, and our prayers must all be mixed with the merits of Jesus' righteousness in order to be accepted by God. Without His righteousness, represented by the gift of frankincense brought by the wise men from the East, our Christian experience is valueless. It is made efficacious only when intermingled with Jesus' righteousness.

What about the gold? What was it prophesying about? Gold is the most precious and costly of metals. It over layered or was the base material for every article that was used in the ancient Jewish sanctuary. The altars, the posts, the seven-branch candlestick, the utensils, and the mercy seat were all composed of gold. Everything in and about the ancient sanctuary was pointing to Jesus and His ministry for salvation for the family. The gold represented his sovereignty over all creation.

In ancient times, gold was the gift that someone would give to a king in recognition of his position of power and prestige. For example, we read about the Queen of Sheba coming to visit King Solomon. The Bible declares, "And she came to Jerusalem with a very great train, with camels that bare spices, and very much GOLD, and precious stones: and when she was come to Solomon, she communed with him of all that was in her heart" (2 Kings 10:2).

Babylon, the territory from which the wise men came, was represented by gold in the mysterious dream of King Nebuchadnezzar. Troubled by a dream which he could not remember; but was convinced of its significance, the king sought the counsel of his wise men to bring the dream back to his memory and to interpret it. None of them was able to perform such a task. But Daniel, the young Hebrew captive, under the inspiration of Creator God, was able to bring the king's dream to his remembrance and gave him the interpretation. Daniel related to the king of Babylon, "Thou, O king, art a king of kings: for the God of heaven hath given thee a kingdom, power, and strength, and glory. And wheresoever the children of men dwell, the beasts of the field and the fowls of the heaven hath He given into thine hand, and hath made thee ruler over them all. Thou art this head of gold" (Daniel 2:37-38).

The gold of the wise men prophesied of our Savior as the King of kings. He is pictured as returning to planet earth with a crown of gold upon His head. John the Revelator declares, "And I looked, and behold a white cloud, and upon the cloud one sat like unto the Son of man, having on his head a golden crown, and in his hand a sharp sickle" (Revelation 14:14).

The wise men of the east were foretelling that the Babe of Bethlehem will give His life as the Lamb slain from the foundations of the world (Revelation 13:8). They were prophesying of the need of the merits of Jesus' ever-present righteousness in the Christian's life. The learned Babylonians were alerting humanity to His glorious second coming as the Lion of the tribe of Judah—no Roman sword to puncture his side, no rusty nails to pierce His hands and feet, no one to spit in His face, no one to mock Him, no crown of thorns upon His head. He would indeed be coming as Lord of lords and King of kings. John declares, "And he hath on his vesture and on his thigh a name written, King Of Kings, And Lord Of Lord" (Revelation 19:16).

As you go through the unavoidable Easter and Christmas seasons, I say to you rejoice. Rejoice as you let somebody know that the Babe of Bethlehem has grown up, lived a sinless life as an example for us to follow. Let them know that as the wise men from the east had prophesied with the myrrh, that He gave His life as a ransom for you and for them. Share with them the fact that as the wise men from the east had foretold of His High Priestly ministry with the gift of the frankincense, that they can come to Him and talk with Him about all their burdens and cares. Let somebody know that He is coming soon, as the wise men prophesied with their gift of gold, as King of kings and Lord of lords. He is coming to take us home to spend the ceaseless ages of eternity with Him in a place where there will be no more death, no more crying, nor sorrow, nor pain, for the former things would have passed away" (Revelation 21:5).

I plan on being there, what about you? He is coming soon to redeem His children for He is the One who died for every member of the human family. That's the rest of the story.

Chapter 7

THE GREAT I AM

There are many things that are written about Jesus Christ in and out of the Bible. Both the Old and the New Testaments have quite a lot to say about Him. The prophets, patriarchs and apostles have all had their say concerning Him and have left us an indelible record of His life and ministry. But none have more forcibly and with greater conviction spoke of Him

God had delivered the Israelites, His chosen people, after four hundred years, from Egyptian captivity. He led them to their encampment in the Sinai Peninsula, far out of the reach of their oppressors. Through the hands of His servant Moses, Jehovah had saved His people from the destructive influence of the Egyptians and provided them a refuge.

Moses was born a Hebrew. Having been miraculously saved as a baby from the Pharaoh's edict to destroy all the newly born Hebrew males, Moses was adopted and raised as an Egyptian by the Pharaoh's daughter. He, in effect, went from slavery to royalty. Moses would eventually rise to become the second in command to the pharaoh, the supreme ruler of Egypt. In the process of time, through some divinely appointed circumstances, He became aware of his Hebrew heritage. He was moved with deep compassion and an overbearing sense of responsibility as he saw his people suffering under rod of the Egyptian taskmasters.

Upon witnessing the merciless flogging of a helpless, aged Hebrew, Moses confronted the oppressor and slew him. Fearing for his own life, he departed Egypt and dwelt in the land of Media several miles away. He became connected with the Priest/King of the Median kingdom, married his eldest daughter and settled into the occupation of a shepherd. He had, in short order, transitioned from royal prince to humble sheep herder.

Forty years had passed when Moses had an encounter that would change not only his life; but that of his people and ultimately, the course of human history. That encounter was with the God of the Hebrews. Whilst tending the flock of his father-in-law, Jethro, Moses came upon a strange scene. It was unlike any he had seen before. He observed, naturally with great amazement and deep curiosity, a fire that was burning in the bushes, but the bushes were not consumed. As he drew closer, Moses heard a voice speaking to him and realized that it was the voice of the God of his people and of his fathers. Having identified Himself to Moses, God revealed to him the mission for which he had chosen him to accomplish—to deliver His people from Egyptian bondage. God explained to Moses,

"Come now therefore and I will send thee unto Pharaoh, that thou mayest bring forth My people, the children of Israel out of Egypt" (Exodus 3:10).

Moses not only began to question God's requirements of him; but related to God all the reasons why he was unable to go on the appointed mission. But God assured Moses of a victorious enterprise by overcoming all his objections. In questioning God's purpose for his life, Moses asked, "Behold, when I come unto the children of Israel, and shall say unto them, The God of your fathers hath sent me unto you; and they shall say to me, what is his name? What shall I say unto them?" God responded, "I AM that I AM...Thus shalt thou say unto the children of Israel, I AM hath sent me unto you" (Exodus 3:13-14). After raising a few more objections, all of which God overcame, Moses went on to accomplish a successful mission in the power of Jesus Christ, the Great I AM.

It would be almost fifteen hundred years later and Moses, along with all those whom God had empowered him to deliver from Egyptian bondage, had passed off the stage of human history. It was then that Jesus Christ, the promised Messiah, whom Moses, the prophets and patriarchs had talked and written about, would appear. However, most of the leaders of Israel would not accept Him for whom He claimed to be. In fact, they continually sought for ways to discredit, confront and malign Him. On one such occasion, Jesus made it abundantly clear to them who He truly was.

Jesus, as He so often did, was appealing to the religious leaders that if they would only believe in Him, He would set them free. The proud leaders boldly retorted that they are the children of Abraham, are not in bondage and therefore have no need to be set free. Jesus countered, to their utter consternation, that Abraham not only desired, but rejoiced to see Him. Of course, both they and Jesus were referring to the Old Testament patriarch through whom God had promised to bring the Messiah. Such a declaration from Jesus raised the ire of the Jews who passionately inquired of Jesus how could He had seen Abraham considering the fact that He [Jesus] was not even fifty years old.

Jesus alarmed them by informing them that He was verily the One who spoke to Moses on the Mount Horeb amidst the burning bush. His response was so abhorrent to them that they gathered stones to stone Him to death. They realized that the very name Creator God revealed to Moses in the burning bush, Jesus declared Himself to be. For Jesus exclaimed to the Jews, "Before Abraham was, I AM" (John 8:58).

Jesus Christ, the Great I AM, the One from everlasting to everlasting, repeatedly expounded on who He truly was during His sojourn on planet earth. He once encountered a woman who came to draw water from a well where He was seated under the blistering heat of the noonday sun. Jesus tactfully began engaging her in conversation. He informed her that He has water to give her and if she would drink of it she will never thirst again and would have everlasting life.

The woman was curiously amazed at His offer. First, she noticed that He had no container with which to draw water from the well. Secondly, she was a Samaritan. This was a group of people with whom the Jews had no dealings. Jesus of course was a Jew. Further, Jesus, whom she had never met before, began to unveil the story of her entire life in a manner that convinced her that He knew her intimately. She soon realized that the person with whom she was speaking was no ordinary man. She did, however, realized that they had one thing in common. She was also of the seed of Abraham and, not unlike the Jews, looked forward to the promised Messiah. She expressed this thought to Jesus. He fondly responded, "I that speak unto thee, AM He" (John4:26).

The woman became so excited that she dropped her water pot and returned to her village to inform her friends and neighbors that she had met the Messiah. Many of her villagers responded by immediately coming to meet Jesus. Upon realizing that her words were true, they invited Him to spend the next two days with them. He accepted their invitation and many more believed on Him for who He said He was--the Messiah, the Great I AM.

Besides those Samaritans, there were many others who believed that Jesus was indeed the Great I AM. Among them was the family of Mary, Martha and

Lazarus. They were very closely attached to Jesus. Their friendship was more akin to family than friends. Sadly, Lazarus, the brother of Mary and Martha, fell ill and eventually died.

Being the itinerant, ever moving evangelist that He was, Jesus was away from their village preaching the kingdom of God when the word got to Him that His good friend was sick. Jesus did not appear to be deeply concerned about the news of the sickness of His very close friend. In fact, He continued His mission for another four days before He came to Bethany, the village of His friend, Lazarus, and his sisters Mary and Martha. By this time, Lazarus was dead and buried. Upon hearing of the approach of Jesus, Martha, with tears in her eyes and pain her heart, hurriedly made her way down the dusty village road to meet Jesus. When she got to Him, she fell at His feet. To Him she expressed the deepest sorrow of her heart coupled with the greatest hope of her life. She cried out to Jesus, "If you had been here, my brother would not have died, but...I know that he shall rise again in the resurrection at the last day". Jesus responded with these words of assurance and comfort, "I AM the resurrection, and the life: he that believeth in Me, though he were dead, yet shall he live" (John 11:21, 24-25).

He then inquired where his friend Lazarus was buried. Upon finding out the location, Jesus proceeded to resurrect him from the grave. He thus declared and demonstrated that He is the Life Giver, the Great I AM.

In His purposeful efforts to convince His hearers, particularly the Jewish leaders, of His true identity, position and purpose, Jesus was rejected at every turn. Nevertheless, to those that accepted Him, He was indeed the Great I AM. They believed, as He said of Himself, I AM the Light of the world and that those that follow Him would not walk in darkness but would have the Light of Life (John 10:12 . When those that followed Him and witnessed His feeding the five thousand with five loaves and two fishes, His declaration, "I AM the Living Bread that came down from heaven and if they partake of it they will live forever were comforting words indeed (John 6:51). To the shepherds who flocked to hear Him, Jesus uttered these words of consolation, "I AM the Good Shepherd" (John 10:11). His revelation that He would give His life for them was the testimony that He was none other than the Great I AM. His pronouncement, "I AM the door: by Me if any man enter in, he shall be saved, and shall go in and out, and find pasture" (John 10:9) gave them further assurance of who He truly is, the Great I AM.

He is appealing to all today, "I amAM the true vine, and my Father is the husbandman. Every branch in me that beareth not fruit he taketh away: and every branch that beareth fruit, he purgeth it, that it may bring forth more fruit (John 15:1-3).

As with Moses on the Mount Horeb, the woman at the well along with her entire village, Martha, Mary and Lazarus in Bethany, the company at the feeding of the five thousand, the shepherds and those who accept Him today, He assures us, "I AM the way, the truth, and the life: no man cometh unto the Father, but by Me" (John 14:6). He is the Great I AM, the One who died for you.

Chapter 8

THE BLESSED HOPE

*M*any are concerned about all that is going on in the world today. There are wars, rumors of wars, pestilences, unusual weather patterns, economic uncertainty, and moral declension. They wonder, what do all these things mean? People are asking, where's the world headed? How will it all end? Does anyone have the answers to the world's problems? Humanity is dismayed and confused. Is there hope for humanity and the planet we occupy?

It has been referred to as the Christian's greatest hope. From the prophets and patriarchs of old, to the early church, to the Protestant Reformers, the visible, literal, and glorious coming of Jesus Christ has been their most cherished expectation. Unfortunately, however, the Blessed Hope seems to have become a lost relic to most of Christendom. Instead, a plethora of human philosophies and false ecclesiastical inventions have taken its place. Was the early church wrong? Has God changed His mind, or, are His people being woefully deceived?

As we look around the world today, we can surely see the signs, predicted by our Lord and Savior, Jesus Christ, which He foretold would occur just prior to His return to planet earth. Even though the reality of Jesus' coming has been distorted or lost its appeal to many Christians, the word of God remains steadfast and sure. Rather than abdicating their faith in the Blessed Hope, Christians should instead be encouraged, strengthened, and rejoice as they see those signs come to pass before their very eyes. His promise to His disciples is simple: "And when these things begin to come to pass, then look up and lift up your heads for your redemption draweth nigh" (Luke 21:28).

When asked by His disciples about the signs of His second coming and of end of the world, Jesus warned them that deception will be one of the greatest signs. Deception is believing something to be true when it is indeed false. So, Jesus' first response to their question was, "Take heed that no man deceive you...For many shall come in my name, saying, I am Christ; and shall deceive many" (Matthew 24:4-5). He went on to talk about the other signs including persecution of the faithful. But; it was deception that He emphatically focused upon. He reiterated to His disciples back then and to Christians today, "And many false prophets shall rise, and shall deceive many" (Matthew 24:11).

As though He wanted them and us to be extra careful of the severity of end-time deceptions, He repeated a third time, "For there shall arise false Christs, and false prophets, and shall shew great signs and wonders; insomuch that, if it were possible, they shall deceive the very elect" (Matthew 24:24). Indeed, Jesus, looking down through the corridor of time, thought it most important and significant to warn His people about strong delusions pertaining to His second coming.

Perhaps, the strongest delusions he foresaw and warned about is the popular teaching of the Secret Rapture. This is a human invention which promotes the idea that at some time, in the not too distant future, all Christians will secretly disappear from earth, supposedly going to heaven, with non-Christians left upon the earth. By misquoting, misunderstanding, and manipulating a few passages of Scripture, this theory has been palmed off to God's people as Bible truth. Neither the prophets of old, Jesus nor His apostles taught such a concept. It cannot be found anywhere in a plain "thus saith the Lord". Not even in the recent history of the mighty Protestant Reformation, was such an idea remotely contemplated. Nevertheless, untold millions of Christians, of both leaders and laity, believe, preach, and teach this heresy.

The Savior Himself foretells, "Immediately after the tribulation of those days shall the sun be darkened, and the moon shall not give her light, and the stars shall fall from heaven, and the powers of the heavens shall be shaken: And then shall appear the sign of the Son of man in heaven: and then shall all the tribes of the earth mourn, and they shall see the Son of man coming in the clouds of heaven with power and great glory. And he shall send his angels with a great sound of a trumpet, and they shall gather together his elect from the four winds, from one end of heaven to the other" (Matthew 24:29-31).

The Gospel writer Luke shares the testimony of the angels, "And while they looked steadfastly toward heaven as He went up, behold, two men stood by them in white apparel; which also said, Ye men of Galilee, why stand ye gazing up into heaven? this same Jesus, which is taken up from you into heaven, shall so come in like manner as ye have seen him go into heaven" (Acts 1:10-11).

The question, therefore, that must be addressed is this, 'where is the idea of the Secret Rapture in the testimony of the angels, the prophets, the apostles, or Jesus Himself'? Of course, it cannot be found. No wonder, Jesus was so intensely focused on the subject of deception when asked by His disciples about His second coming. But then again, by being deceived one does not know that he or she is imbibing error.

Happily, God has provided a way to be undeceived. He beckons us through His servant Paul, "Study to shew thyself approved unto God, a workman that needeth not to be ashamed, rightly dividing the word of truth" (2 Timothy 2:15). The learned apostle further gives the reason why God's people must individually study His word for themselves and not be deceived by the philosophies of learned men so-called and the pronouncements of ecclesiastical councils. He concurs with his Master, Jesus Christ, "For such are false apostles, deceitful workers, transforming themselves into the apostles of Christ. And no marvel; for Satan himself is transformed into an angel of light. Therefore it is no great thing if his ministers also be transformed as the ministers of righteousness; whose end shall be according to their works" (2 Corinthians 11:13-15).

Both Jesus and Paul, along with others in the early church, must have foresaw a time when false teachings and deceptions would characterize people's understanding of the word of God, particularly with regards to the Blessed Hope. So, Paul counsels and comforts the believers, "Behold, I shew you a mystery; we shall not all sleep, but we shall all be changed. In a moment, in the twinkling of an eye, at the last trump: for the trumpet shall sound, and the dead shall be raised incorruptible, and we shall be changed. For this corruptible must put on incorruption, and this mortal must put on immortality. So, when this corruptible shall have put on incorruption, and this mortal shall have put on immortality, then shall be brought to pass the saying that is written, Death is swallowed up in victory" (1 Corinthians 15:51-54).

Please take careful note that we get immortality at the second coming of Jesus Christ, not one second before. We do not have it now, neither do our dear, loved ones who have fallen asleep. They are simply sleeping in their graves, like Lazarus of old, awaiting the call of the Life Giver, Jesus Christ Himself. They are waiting to go on the greatest vacation ever, along with those who will be alive and remain when Jesus comes.

The Blessed Hope, the visible, literal, glorious appearing of our Lord and Savior, Jesus Christ, is certain. The ancients looked forward to it. For example, the patriarch Job, finding himself in the most despicable physical human condition any human being can experience, declared, "For I know that my Redeemer liveth, and that He shall stand at the latter day upon the earth: And though after my skin worms destroy this body, yet in my flesh shall I see God: Whom I shall see for myself, and mine eyes shall behold, and not another; though my reins be consumed within me" (Job 19:25-27).

The apostle Paul wrote to his Hebrew countrymen to help them understand that Jesus Christ is indeed the promised Messiah to whom they looked forward. He referred to their father Abraham showing that he [Abraham] steadfastly looked forward to the Blessed Hope. Paul declared, "By faith he sojourned in the land of promise, as in a strange country, dwelling in tabernacles with Isaac and Jacob, the heirs with him of the same promise: For he looked for a city which hath foundations, whose builder and maker is God" (Hebrews 11:9-10). God's dedicated evangelist, then talked about the great heroes of the Christian faith and summed up their singular belief thus, "But now they desire a better country, that is, an heavenly: wherefore God is not ashamed to be called their God: for he hath prepared for them a city" (Hebrews 11:16).

King David exclaimed, "Our God shall come, and shall not keep silence: a fire shall devour before him, and it shall be very tempestuous round about him" (Psalms 50:3). Likewise, the promise of that glorious appearing was not lost on His beloved disciple John. He exclaimed, "Behold, He cometh with clouds; and every eye shall see him, and they also which pierced him: and all kindreds of the earth shall wail because of him. Even so, Amen" (Revelation 1:7).

John continued, "And I saw heaven opened, and behold a white horse; and he that sat upon him was called Faithful and True, and in righteousness he doth judge and make war. His eyes were as a flame of fire, and on his head were many crowns; and he had a name written, that no man knew, but He himself. And he was clothed with a vesture dipped in blood: and his name is called The Word of God. And the armies which were in heaven followed him upon white horses, clothed in fine linen, white and clean. And out of his mouth goeth a sharp sword, that with it he should smite the nations: and he shall rule them with a rod of iron: and he treadeth the winepress of the fierceness and wrath of Almighty God. And he hath on his vesture and on his thigh a name written, King of Kings, And Lord of Lords" (Revelation 19:11-16).

God promised it. The patriarchs and prophets believed it. The early church proclaimed it. The angels comfort us with it. But most of all, our Savior assures us of it. On the night preceding His fateful journey to Calvary's cross, Jesus gathered with His disciples to have a final meal with them. He gave them their marching orders and assured them of victory in their mission. But they were saddened by the fact that He was about to depart from them. Recognizing their bewilderment, He offered these words of comfort to them back then and to us today, "Let not your heart be troubled: ye believe in God, believe also in me. In my Father's house are many mansions: if it were not so, I would have told you. I go to prepare a place for you. And if I go and prepare a place for you, I will come again, and receive you unto myself; that where I am, there ye may be also" (John 14:1-3).

Again, the apostle Paul makes the Blessed Hope his focal point in outlining the plan of human redemption to the young minister, Titus. He wrote, "For the grace of God that bringeth salvation hath appeared to all men, Teaching us that, denying ungodliness and worldly lusts, we should live soberly, righteously, and godly, in this present world; Looking for that blessed hope, and the glorious appearing of the great God and our Savior Jesus Christ" (Titus 2:11-13)

But how certain can we be of His coming? As the world crumbles from the weight of sin, the Christian must have faith in that Blessed Hope. Now is not the time to get discouraged, fearful, and despondent. For not too distant, the heavens will roll back like a scroll and the Lord will descend.

Men may be deceived by popular fiction and grandiose, money-making Hollywood productions; but God has not changed His mind. The patriarchs, prophets, early church, and Protestant Reformers all had it right. Be faithful and true to His word and He shall grant you a crown of eternal life and an existence of immortal glory.

Considering the evidence of all the other events prophesied about Him and fulfilled in His life, you can be confident that indeed this final event, the Blessed Hope, will be likewise fulfilled as prophesied. Jesus Christ, the Creator of the world (John 1:1-3, 14) can be trusted when He implores us that He will come again to rescue humanity from this world of sin, perplexity, and woe. We can have faith in His word when He promises to make all things new.

To date, everything that He had promised and that which had been prophesied about Him, by the prophets of old, have come to pass exactly as was foretold. When and where He would be born, the precise period He would do His ministry on earth, how, when and where He would die have all been fulfilled with divine precision. With such an impeccable record, we can join voices with the apostle Paul when he says, "Henceforth there is laid up for me a crown of righteousness, which the Lord, the righteous judge, shall give me at that day:

and not to me only, but unto all them also that love his appearing" (2 Timothy 4:8).

When that day comes the entire world will be divided into two classes. One class is described thus, "And the kings of the earth, and the great men, and the rich men, and the chief captains, and the mighty men, and every bondman, and every free man, hid themselves in the dens and in the rocks of the mountains; And said to the mountains and rocks, Fall on us, and hide us from the face of him that sitteth on the throne, and from the wrath of the Lamb: For the great day of his wrath is come; and who shall be able to stand? (Revelation 6:15-17).

But, the other class, the one I pray that you and I will be in, will look up, face to face with our Savior, and joyfully declare, "Lo, this is our God; we have waited for him, and he will save us: this is the Lord; we have waited for him, we will be glad and rejoice in his salvation" (Isaiah 25:9). He shall then respond with the most melodious voice ever heard in human ears, "Come, ye blessed of my Father, inherit the kingdom prepared for you from the foundation of the world" (Matthew 25:34). My sincere prayer is that we will all be in that class. Hold fast to the Blessed Hope. It is assured by the One who died for you.

Chapter 9

THE GREATEST VACATION EVER

$\mathcal{V}$acations are always wonderful occasions. Much time is spent selecting the destination. The best travel and hotel deals are sought after. There is careful planning as the raw excitement about visiting a new place grows ever fonder. Whether the destination is near or far, the very thought of taking a break from one's daily routine and the stresses of everyday life bring joy to the heart. Seldom can one resist the temptation to let everyone know that they are going on vacation. In fact, people relish in sharing the great news.

But what if your upcoming vacation would be the greatest one you would ever have? How would you prepare for it? How much joy would it bring to your heart and how many people would you tell about it? Of course, that would depend on how excited you are and how much you are looking forward to that vacation. I invite you to consider what is the greatest vacation you could ever have. I pray that you would become excited about it and treat it with at least the same fervor as your other vacations.

Not too long ago I was looking at a documentary, on a major television network, focusing on end-time events. A leading televangelist, who was a featured guest on this program, was talking about the Millennium. In one segment, he referred to the millennium with Jesus as a time of peace and bliss upon the earth for God's people. In the very next segment, out of the same lips, this leading evangelical declared that God's people could be 'raptured' away from the earth at any second now. He went on to relate that having being raptured away, God's people will have the opportunity to see the subsequent destruction that would take place on the earth.

I wondered to myself, 'what Bible does this dear man read? Of course, his pronouncements are what are parroted by both 'leaders' and followers alike in the Christian world. Even without any Bible knowledge, one can easily discern that such teachings, taken together, are inherently contradictory and patently confusing. How can one be raptured away, witness the destruction of the wicked and the planet, and at the same time enjoy a thousand years of bliss upon the earth? Our God is not a God of confusion. By His grace, we shall show from the Bible, what God really says about the Millennium. In fact, from God's perspective, you will discover that the Millennium will be the greatest vacation you could ever have.

The word 'Millennium' does not appear in the Bible. It is a combination of two Latin words: 'milli', meaning one thousand; and 'annum', meaning year. Most Christians understand that the Millennium is a reference to the thousand-year period mentioned in the book of Revelation.

There is no dispute that there will be a millennium of peace and unspeakable bliss for God's people. The problem arises when one tries to determine where this experience will take place. Some say that it occurs upon the earth. Others contend that it takes place in heaven. In this discourse, we will find out, from God's word, what is the Millennium, where and when it takes place, and what happens, before, during and after it occurs.

It must always be borne in mind that God's Plan of Salvation is revealed to us in an unbroken chain of divine truth that fits perfectly together. Each link connecting in a seamless bond with the next. Any teaching that does not fit into that chain must be rejected.

It is impossible to reconcile the Secret Rapture with a thousand years of bliss upon the earth, as that famous evangelical and so many others believe. Both concepts are erroneous, deceptive, and dangerous. Neither fits into God's perfect, self-defining Plan of Redemption for men's souls as is presented in that unbroken chain of divine truth. But how does the Millennium fit into that unbroken chain? Indeed, where will you spend your greatest vacation ever?

The apostle Paul teaches us clearly what happens when Jesus returns. He writes, 'For this we say unto you by the word of the Lord, that we which are alive and remain unto the coming of the Lord shall not prevent them which are asleep...For the Lord Himself shall descend from heaven with a shout, with the voice of the Archangel, and with the trump of God: and the dead in Christ shall rise first; then we which are alive and remain shall be caught up together with them in the clouds, to meet the Lord in the air: and so shall we ever be with the Lord" (1 Thessalonians 4:15-17). John concurs: "Behold, He cometh with clouds; and every eye shall see him, and they also which pierced him: and all kindreds of the earth shall wail because of him. Even so, Amen" (Revelation 1:7).

Several points are made in these passages:

Jesus Christ will be returning visibly with a great noise. No secret here.

1) He will be returning for His saints.

2) The dead (sleeping) righteous will be resurrected

3) The living saints will be caught up with them to meet the Lord in the air.

4) All the righteous, resurrected and living, will be transformed into immortal glory and go with the Lord back to heaven. The greatest vacation ever, the Millennium, begins.

John seamlessly connects the next perfectly fitted link to God's unbroken chain of divine truth. He assures us, "And I saw thrones, and they sat upon them, and judgment was given unto them: and I saw the souls of them that were beheaded for the witness for Jesus, and for the word of God, and which had not worshipped the beast, neither his image, neither had received his mark upon their foreheads, or in their hands; and they lived and reigned with Christ a thousand years...But the rest of the dead lived not until the thousand years were finished. This is the first resurrection...Blessed and holy is he that hath part in the first resurrection: on such the second death hath power, but they shall be priests of God and of Christ, and shall reign with Him a thousand years" (Revelation 20:4-6). So simple: Jesus returns for the saints, takes them home with Him to heaven to spend a thousand years, the greatest vacation we will ever have.

So much for God's people. Now, let's take an inspired look at the fate of the wicked. First, the wicked dead will already be dead. But what will happen to the wicked living when Jesus returns? Paul again answers: "Now we beseech you, bretheren, by the coming of our Lord Jesus Christ, and by our gathering together unto Him...and then shall the wicked be revealed, whom the Lord shall consume with the spirit of His mouth and shall destroy with the brightness of His coming...And with all deceivableness of unrighteousness in them that perish; because they received not the love of the truth, that they might be saved" (2 Thessalonians 2:1, 8, 10).

John adds more detail to the picture. He reveals, "And I saw an angel come down from heaven, having the key of the bottomless pit and a great chain in his hand. And he laid hold on the dragon, that old serpent, which is the Devil, and Satan, and bound him a thousand years, And cast him into the bottomless pit, and shut him up, and set a seal upon him, that he should deceive the nations no more, till the thousand years should be fulfilled: and after that he must be loosed a little season" (Revelation 20:-3).

The Gospel prophet Isaiah is in perfect harmony with John. He foretold, "And they shall be gathered together, as prisoners are gathered in the pit, and shall be shut up in the prison, and after many days shall they be visited" (Isaiah 24:22). The ancient seer, Jeremiah, describes the prison in which the wicked, all dead, will be shut up. He also prophesied, "And the slain of the Lord shall be at that day from one end of the earth even unto the other end of the earth: they shall not be lamented, neither gathered, nor buried; they shall be dung upon the ground" (Jeremiah 25:33).

In addition to the plain teachings of Paul and other New Testament writers on the fate of the saved and unsaved when Jesus returns; we have great insight on the condition of the earth at Jesus' coming and during the Millennium, from the prophets of old.

Jeremiah writes, " I beheld the earth, and, lo, it was without form, and void; and the heavens and they had no light...I beheld the mountains, and, lo, they trembled, and all the hills moved lightly...I beheld, and lo, there was no man, and all the birds of the heaven were fled... I beheld, and lo, the fruitful place was a wilderness, and all the cities thereof were broken down at the presence of the Lord and by His fierce anger...For thus hath the Lord said: the whole land shall be desolate; yet will I not make a full end" (Jeremiah 4:23-27).

Again, the prophet Isaiah agrees completely. He states, "The land shall be utterly emptied, and utterly spoiled: for the Lord hath spoken His word. The earth mourneth and fadeth away, the world languisheth and fadeth away, the haughty people of the earth do languish...Fear, and the pit, and the snare are upon thee, O inhabitants of the earth...The earth is utterly broken down, the earth is clean dissolved, the earth is moved exceedingly" (Isaiah 24: 3-5, 17,19). Notice the consistency and similarity with Jeremiah's account, Isaiah's account and John's account. Quite remarkable, isn't it? No time of peace and bliss upon the earth, only utter destruction and desolation.

Isaiah and Jeremiah declare that after all the destruction and devastation of the earth, the wicked slain would be 'visited' But what are they talking about? John answers, "And when the thousand years are expired, Satan shall be loosed out of his prison" (Revelation 20:7). The wicked dead are now resurrected.

This is the second resurrection. John continues, "And the sea gave up the dead which were in it: and death and hell delivered up the dead which were in them; and they were judged every man according to his works" (Revelation 20:13).

Satan is now loosed out of his prison by virtue of the fact that he now has people to tempt and deceive. For one thousand years he was locked up in his prison of circumstances, *i.e.* no one to tempt into rebellion against the God of creation. He was bound in the nothingness of the devastated earth. But now, after the thousand years, his circumstances change. The wicked are now resurrected and the devil deceives them just as he did during their lifetime. He convinces the now resurrected wicked that they can capture and overtake the New Jerusalem as it descends to the earth with the redeemed, returning from the greatest vacation they have ever had.

It has always been the devil's desire to take the place of God. Talking of Lucifer, before he became Satan, Isaiah declares, "For thou hast said in thine heart, I will ascend into heaven, I will exalt my throne above the stars of God: I will sit also upon the mount of the congregation, in the sides of the north: I will ascend above the heights of the clouds; I will be like the most High" (Isaiah 14: 13-14). But then the prophet foretells Satan's fate: "Yet thou shalt be brought down to hell, to the sides of the pit" (Isaiah 14:15).

John elaborates, "And they (the devil and his armies of resurrected wicked) shall go out to deceive the nations which are in the four corners of the earth, Gog and Magog to gather together to battle: the number of whom is as the sand of the sea...And they went up on the breath of the earth, and compassed the camp of the saints about, and the beloved city: and fire came down from heaven, and devoured them...death and hell were cast into the lake of fire. This is the second death...and whosoever was not found written in the book of life was cast into the lake of fire" (Revelation 20:14-15).

The terms Gog and Magog are used here symbolically, as do much of the images in the book of Revelation. They do not refer to the literal nations of Old Testament times. Historically, Gog and Magog were nations that fiercely fought against God's people. They were ultimately eradicated by Israel. The symbolism is quite fitting for the final battle of the ages. (See Ezekiel chapters 38, 39).

The fire that destroys the wicked is the same fire that purifies the earth from sin and makes it ready for habitation of God's redeemed.

The prophet Zechariah describes this event: "and this shall be the plague wherewith the Lord will smite all the people that have fought against Jerusalem; Their flesh shall consume away while they stand upon their feet, and their eyes shall consume away in their holes, and their tongue shall consume away in their mouth"

(Zechariah 14:12). He also states, "And His (Jesus) feet shall stand in that day upon the mount of Olives, which is before Jerusalem on the east, and the mount of Olives shall cleave in the midst thereof toward the west, and there shall be a very great valley; and half of the mountain shall remove toward the north, and half toward the south" (Zechariah 14:4).

The vacation now ends and the saints are returned to their home—the earth made new. The Millennium is a vacation like none other. You won't dread its end. No disgust is felt as you prepare to return home. It's a vacation that never ends; for it returns the redeemed to a recreated earth in its Edenic form. Jesus teaches, "Blessed are the meek for they shall inherit the earth" (Matthew 5:5).

Isaiah gives us a glimpse of our new home when we return from vacation, "The wolf also shall dwell with the lamb, and the leopard shall lie down with the kid; and the calf and the young lion and the fatling together; and a little child shall lead them. And the cow and the bear shall feed; their young ones shall lie down together: and the lion shall eat straw like the ox. And the sucking child shall play on the hole of the asp, and the weaned child shall put his hand on the cockatrice' den" (Isaiah 11:6-8).

John the Revelator makes it even plainer, "And I saw a new heaven and a new earth: for the first heaven and the first earth were passed away; and there was no more sea. And I John saw the holy city, new Jerusalem, coming down from God out of heaven, prepared as a bride adorned for her husband. And I heard a great voice out of heaven saying, Behold, the tabernacle of God is with men, and he will dwell with them, and they shall be his people, and God himself shall be with them, and be their God. And God shall wipe away all tears from their eyes; and there shall be no more death, neither sorrow, nor crying, neither shall there be any more pain: for the former things are passed away. And he that sat upon the throne said, Behold, I make all things new. And he said unto me, Write: for these words are true and faithful (Revelation 21:1-5).

This is the word of God.

1) Jesus comes visibly, literally and with a great shout to gather His saints and take us to heaven.

2) We live with Him in heaven for one thousand years.   (The Millennium, the greatest vacation ever begins.)

3) The wicked are dead and are scattered across the face of the destroyed, desolate earth.

4) During that time the earth is broken, void and uninhabited. No life on earth. This is Satan's prison, he has no one to temp.

5) At the end of the thousand years, the wicked dead are resurrected only to continue in their

wickedness by attempting to capture the City of God, New Jerusalem.

6) Fire comes down from heaven and devours them.

7) The same fire that destroys the wicked also purifies the earth and makes it new for God's people to enjoy throughout eternity.

8) Sin and sinners are no more.

What a perfect plan and a glorious day. God, according to His plan, takes care of the sin problem and all its blighted effects. You need not be deceived by man's erroneous theories. Your salvation must be based upon the word of God and not man's smartness. The visible, literal Second Coming of Christ fits like a hand in glove with the Biblical teaching of the Millennium. There is no schism. No confusion surrounds it. Such are all the doctrines that comprise God's plan of Redemption for men's souls. They are indeed knitted into a golden chain of unified, divine truth.

Unlike the errors of the Secret Rapture and a Millennium of peace on earth, God's word gives us light. It provides clear direction and sets us free from human tradition and deceptive inventions. Paul's counsel to us in this area is thus: "Wherefore comfort one another with these words" (1 Thessalonians 4:18).

May you become excited and tell someone of the greatest vacation you will ever have. My sincere prayer is that you prepare for that vacation and tell as many as you can about it. It will indeed be the greatest vacation you will ever have because you'll spend it with the One who died for you.

Chapter 10

THE FINAL SUPERPOWER

*T*he world is filled with wars and rumors of wars. It appears a new conflict is breaking out by the second. There is conflagration on every corner of planet earth. Nation is revolting against nation. Culture is warring against culture. Tribe is rising against tribe. Additionally, there is unrelenting moral and social declension. Diseases and pestilences are rampant. Economic collapse seems to be lurking around the corner. Nature has strayed from its appointed course. It is verily just as Jesus Christ predicted it would be before His second coming (Matthew 24:6-7).

Religious leaders, politicians and statesmen offer their remedies for the apparently insurmountable problems that confront the human family. Yet none have the answer to mankind's seemingly inescapable predicament. The world appears to be heading to its date with a destructive destiny.

In the midst of all this, speculation abounds as to who will be the next superpower. Will America continue indefinitely in that capacity? Will China out maneuver her and usurp her position? Will Radical Islam succeed in its push for world domination? And, Russia, will it succeed in establishing dominance over the nations of the world? Who will ultimately hold sway over the nations of the earth?

The annals of human history are littered with the magnificence of great empires which share a common theme--they rise, dominate, and then they fall. The very document that records these epochs, with their shared DNA, also tells of one kingdom that will arise, not only be more magnificent and glorious than all that have preceded it; but unlike its predecessors, will never fall. It will, the record reveals, last forever. It will be the World's Final Superpower.

That document is the Holy Bible. To some it is simply a collection of ancient fables. To others it is no more than a piece of good literary exposition. Yet, to many, it is the work of Creator God who created all humanity. What's undeniable, however, is its uncannily accurate predictions of the existence and fate of world empires hundreds of years before they appear on the world stage. That very record assures us of the establishment and perpetuity of the World's Final Superpower.

The year was around 606 BC, Babylon, having conquered the Assyrian empire, thereby becoming the world superpower of its time, invaded the Jewish nation and took many of its citizens captive. As was customary of the times, Babylon's ruling monarch, Nebuchadnezzar, seized the brightest, smartest, and strongest of his conquered prey to serve him and help fortify his empire. Among those that he acquired were four very intelligent, God-faring young men who showed great potential of being valuable in the king's court. They were thus given the best treatment and most considerate care that the king could offer. Their Hebrew names were Daniel, Hananiah, Mishael, and Azariah. But King Nebuchadnezzar, in his attempt to fully integrate them into his empire, changed their names to what have now become so recognizable as Belteshazzar, Shadrach, Meshach, and Abendigo.

Not too long after their captivity in Babylon, a crisis arose. The ruling monarch, King Nebuchadnezzar, had a dream which was extremely impressionable, and he thought was of great importance. The king, however, could not remember what he dreamt and demanded of his wise men and astrologers that they must not only tell him what he dreamt; but also give him the interpretation of his dream. To his raging displeasure, the wise men informed the king that such a task was impossible to accomplish. They notified the king that no human being could perform such a feat. An angry and frustrated King Nebuchadnezzar, fiercely determined to remember his dream and have it interpreted, decreed that the wise men must either fulfill his request or have their heads chopped off and their houses burned to ashes.

Daniel, Shadrach, Meshach, and Abendigo, being part of the king's cadre of wise men, now faced the real possibility of experiencing the king's wrath. As word got to them of the impending death decree, Daniel pleaded with the king's chief advisor, Arioch, who was charged with the responsibility of carrying out the king's death decree. Daniel petitioned Arioch to allow him an audience with the monarch. His petition was granted and Daniel was afforded an opportunity to speak with the king. After listening to the king's dilemma, Daniel asked that he be granted some time to commune with his companions and his [Daniel] God who would be able to answer the king's requests.

Upon receiving the king's permission, Daniel met with his three companions. They held a prayer meeting in which they presented the king's petition to their God, asking that He would grant them the wisdom to help the king recall his dream and give him the interpretation thereof. Daniel's God, the God of all creation, not only revealed the king's dream to them, but gave them the interpretation and meaning of it. Daniel surely remembered what his God had told His prophet Isaiah, "Remember the former things of old: for I am God, and there is none else; I am God, and there is none like me, Declaring the end from the beginning, and from ancient times the things that are not yet done, saying, My counsel shall stand, and I will do all my pleasure" (Isaiah 46:9-10).

Daniel returned to the king with the message his God gave to him to share with the king. The powerful monarch was of course excitedly eager to hear what Daniel had to say. God's ambassador began his conversation by telling the king that his God, who knows the beginning from the end and who sets up kings and takes them down, had given him [Nebuchadnezzar] the great kingdom of Babylon over which he ruled. As Daniel proceeded to reveal the king's dream, the ruler grew increasingly attentive, amazed, and relaxed. He showed his amazement even as he expressed agreement. For Daniel related to the king precisely what he dreamt.

Daniel related to Nebuchadnezzar that he dreamt of an image of a man. This was no ordinary image. It was unusually large. The head was of gold. The chest and arms were made of silver. The belly was composed of brass. The legs were constructed of iron. The feet and toes were a comingling of iron and clay. Finally, there was a stone that descended out of the heavens and struck the image on the feet of iron and clay, grinding the gold, silver, brass, iron and the clay into oblivion. No wonder King Nebuchadnezzar had problems remembering his dream. It was an awesome sight. With a great sense of satisfaction and deep appreciation, the king confirmed to Daniel that this was indeed what he had dreamt.

Daniel and his companions then went on to give the king, what none other of his wise men were able to give, the interpretation of the dream. They related to King Nebuchadnezzar: "This is the dream; and we will tell the interpretation thereof before the king. Thou, O king, art a king of kings: for the God of heaven hath given thee a kingdom, power, and strength, and glory. And wheresoever the children of men dwell, the beasts of the field and the fowls of the heaven hath he given into thine hand, and hath made thee ruler over them all. Thou art this head of gold" (Daniel 2:36-38).

They continued, "And after thee shall arise another kingdom inferior to thee, and another third kingdom of brass, which shall bear rule over all the earth. And the fourth kingdom shall be strong as iron: forasmuch as iron breaketh in pieces and subdueth all things: and as iron that breaketh all these, shall it break in pieces and bruise.

They related further, "And whereas thou sawest the feet and toes, part of potters' clay, and part of iron, the kingdom shall be divided; but there shall be in it of the strength of the iron, forasmuch as thou sawest the iron mixed with miry clay. And as the toes of the feet were part of iron, and part of clay, so the kingdom shall be partly strong, and partly broken. And whereas thou sawest iron mixed with miry clay, they shall mingle themselves with the seed of men: but they shall not cleave one to another, even as iron is not mixed with clay.

Then they concluded,   "And in the days of these kings shall the God of heaven set up a kingdom, which shall never be destroyed: and the kingdom shall not be left to other people, but it shall break in pieces and consume all these kingdoms, and it shall stand for ever. Forasmuch as thou sawest that the stone was cut out of the mountain without hands, and that it brake in pieces the iron, the brass, the clay, the silver, and the gold; the great God hath made known to the king what shall come to pass hereafter: and the dream is certain, and the interpretation thereof sure" (Daniel 2:39-45).

What Daniel's God had revealed to the monarch of Babylon through His servants was the history of the world from his [Nebuchadnezzar] time to the end of time as we know it. It would culminate with the second coming of Jesus Christ and His eternal rule in the affairs of men; indeed, the world's Final Superpower.

With the precision that only Creator God can orchestrate, Daniel revealed to the Babylonian monarch the superpowers that would hold sway over the affairs of men. They would take center stage in the drama of human experience at the times of their existence and have a significant impact on God's plan for the salvation of the human family. What was revealed to Nebuchadnezzar was later unveiled to Daniel, who subsequently had his own dreams depicting the same flow of human history. Those epochs have come to pass with unerring accuracy.

Following the capture of Jerusalem and reign of Babylon, 606 BC-536 BC, symbolized by the head of gold; the empire of the Medes and Persians, depicted by the chest and arms of silver, ruled universal from 536 BC to 331 BC. Then arose the Grecian Empire, headed by the famed Alexander the Great, which held universal dominion from 331 BC to 168 BC. The legs of iron is a most fitting representation of the iron monarchy of Rome which seized the scepter and ruled from 168 BC to about the middle of the fifth century AD.

Rome was never conquered by another superpower; but her internal disintegration gave rise to the Roman Papacy, the European Ecclesiastical Establishment that ruled the then known world until its demise in the eighteenth century. Historian writes, "The armies of the state were replaced by the missionaries of the church, moving in all directions along the Roman roads; and the revolted provinces, accepting Christianity, acknowledged the sovereignty of Rome. The church with the shadows of the ancient authority behind it, was the only symbol left of imperial Rome. Its bishop, the Pope of Rome, was the city's only recourse for leadership and protection. The Roman Empire in Europe would be replaced by the spiritual empire, which came to be temporal as well, whose reigning seigneur was the bishop of Rome" (Caesar and Christ, page 672, Will Durant).

The feet and toes of iron intermingled with clay quite aptly describes this condition of church/state union which replaced the disintegrated Imperial Roman Empire. It is the foundational characteristic of the Roman Papacy. The iron is clearly identified as a state entity. But the clay, what does it represent? The prophet Isaiah educates us: "But now, O Lord, thou art our father; we are the clay, and thou our potter; and we all are the work of thy hand" (Isaiah 64:8). The clay here quite plainly refers to a religious entity. But Daniel alludes to the clay of Nebuchadnezzar's dream as miry clay (Daniel 2:42). What then is miry clay? The Psalmist David answers: "He brought me up also out of an horrible pit, out of the miry clay, and set my feet upon a rock, and established my goings" (Psalms 40:2). Miry clay is akin to quicksand. You step into it and you keep going down and down until you suffocate and die. It is also very messy.

Obviously, God's revelation to King Nebuchadnezzar, through His servant Daniel, is that of a universal amalgamation of state powers with false, apostate religions that will permeate the earth just before Jesus comes. For it is at this time, in the era of the feet of iron mixed with miry clay, that the stone that is cut out without hands descends to demolish the entire image (Daniel 2:44).

Jesus, the Rock of All Ages crushes the image, signifying His obliteration of all earthly powers and establishes the Final Superpower--His eternal kingdom. Jesus Christ, the King of kings and Lord of lords is the stone that King Nebuchadnezzar saw in his dream.

The apostle Paul tells us: "And are built upon the foundation of the apostles and prophets, Jesus Christ himself being the chief corner stone" (Ephesians 2:20). His co-laborer Peter concurs: "To whom coming, as unto a living stone, disallowed indeed of men, but chosen of God, and precious. Ye also, as lively stones, are built up a spiritual house, an holy priesthood, to offer up spiritual sacrifices, acceptable to God by Jesus Christ. Wherefore also it is contained in the scripture, Behold, I lay in Sion a chief corner stone, elect, precious: and he that believeth on him shall not be confounded." (1 Peter 2:4-6).

When Jesus returns, ushering the Final Superpower, He indeed will bring peace, justice and equity. We are living in a time when the nations of the world are clasping hands with religions of all characters and essence, with the illusive objective of cementing a universal bond of unity and peace. They are coming together under the aegis of the Roman Papacy. John's prophecy is being fulfilled before our very eyes: 'the whole world is wondering after the beast' (Revelation 13:3). The Roman Papacy is promising peace and justice through the agency of universal church/state union which she is orchestrating. But it cannot and will not deliver. Instead, chaos and tyranny beyond human imagination will be the result. Only Jesus Christ, the Prince of Peace, can bring peace and justice to the human family.

As the confusion and calamities increase, that universal union of state with apostate religion, inspired by the devil himself, will turn their fury upon God's people who, like those in ages past, will take a valiant stand for Him. His servant John describes it thus: "And the dragon was wroth with the woman, and went to make war with the remnant of her seed, which keep the commandments of God, and have the testimony of Jesus Christ" (Revelation 12:17).

But he later assures us, "And the ten horns which thou sawest are ten kings, which have received no kingdom as yet; but receive power as kings one hour with the beast. These have one mind, and shall give their power and strength unto the beast...These shall make war with the Lamb, and the Lamb shall overcome them: for he is Lord of lords, and King of kings: and they that are with him are called, and chosen, and faithful" (Revelation 17: 12-14).

Then John gives us a glimpse of the Final Superpower, which will be established after God's people return from their greatest vacation ever. He joyfully declares, "And I saw a new heaven and a new earth: for the first heaven and the first earth were passed away; and there was no more sea. And I John saw the holy city, New Jerusalem, coming down from God out of heaven, prepared as a bride adorned for her husband. And I heard a great voice out of heaven saying, Behold, the tabernacle of God is with men, and he will dwell with them, and they shall be his people, and God himself shall be with them, and be their God. And God shall wipe away all tears from their eyes; and there shall be no more death, neither sorrow, nor crying, neither shall there be any more pain: for the former things are passed away. And he that sat upon the throne said, Behold, I make all things new. And he said unto me, Write: for these words are true and faithful" (Revelation 21:1-5).

As certainly as Nebuchadnezzar's dream became a reality in human history up to this point, so will the prophecy of John be realized; for John simply offered more details to the king's dream. The conclusion in both cases is the same--Jesus Christ will establish the Final Superpower which will last forever. I invite you to be part of it as the One who died for you will rule over His soon-coming kingdom.

Chapter 11

THE ONLY SURE FOUNDATION

*S*tealthily, but rapidly, the world is being prepared for changes which most are unprepared for. They will be very stormy changes. Pen cannot describe nor tongue utter the scope, magnitude and severity of those changes that would come upon the world as an overwhelming surprise. Late Roman Catholic Jesuit scholar, Malachi Martin, describes those changes thus, "Our way of life as individuals and as citizens of the nations; our families and our jobs; our trade and commerce and money; our educational systems and our religions and our cultures; even the badges of our national identity, which most of us have often taken for granted--all will have powerfully and radically altered forever. No one can be exempted from its effects. No sector of our lives remain untouched" (Keys Of This Blood, Malachi Martin, pg. 15).

But the good news is that there is a shelter from this coming storm. It is the only sure foundation upon which we will be able to stand in the soon coming crisis. We are assured: "I will say of the Lord, He is my refuge and my fortress: my God; in him will I trust. Surely he shall deliver thee from the snare of the fowler, and from the noisome pestilence. He shall cover thee with his feathers, and under his wings shalt thou trust: his truth shall be thy shield and buckler. Thou shalt not be afraid for the terror by night; nor for the arrow that flieth by day; Nor for the pestilence that walketh in darkness; nor for the destruction that wasteth at noonday. A thousand shall fall at thy side, and ten thousand at thy right hand; but it shall not come nigh thee" (Psalm 91:2-7).

The Holy Bible in which we find those comforting and assuring words is both our shelter and our only sure foundation. The Bible, being its own expositor, is unique in its claims about itself and the human condition it portrays. This places it in a class all by itself. It is verily the word of God. All human teachings are subordinate to it. It needs no man's philosophy, theology nor ideology to comprehend its teachings. The Bible is a precious book. It is a unique book, truly like none other. It makes the drunkard sober. It takes the liar and make him truthful. It takes the lady of the night and makes her a jewel in the crown of its author. It makes the profligate honest.

The Bible has been translated into more languages, tongues and dialects than any other book. It is verily the word of God. Its teachings are equally applicable to all classes and cultures. Its timeless nature is beyond human comprehension. One writer declared, "the Bible is an anvil that has worn out many hammers". It is true to the promise of its Author: "The grass withereth, the flower fadeth: but the word of our God shall stand for ever" (Isaiah 40:8).

As we examine the Bible, we discover that there are at least seven elements that prove it to be what it claims to be---the word of Creator God and thus, the Only Sure Foundation.

(1) **Internal Consistency:** The Bible was written over a time span of about 1500 years. It was penned by approximately 40 men from 3 continents. Most of them did not know each other. They hailed from varied socio-economic backgrounds. They embraced varying cultural heritages. They represented diverse life experiences. Despite these variables, all Bible writers relate one inescapable, enduring story. That is the story of God's love for mankind. They all point their readers to the only, omnipotent, merciful God who seeks to restore man back to His (God's) image from which we have fallen. They all, without exception, relate the story of the creation of man, the fall of man and the redemption of man through Jesus Christ, the Only Begotten Son of God. Jesus sums up the story: "For God so loved the world that He gave His only begotten son, that whosoever believeth in Him should not perish, but have everlasting life. For God sent not His Son into the world to condemn the world, but that the world through Him might be saved" (John 3:16-17). No other book or collection of books can match that record.

(2) **Universal Relevancy:** The teachings of the Bible are equally applicable to the human family today as it were to them six thousand years ago. The foundation of not only civil society; but also of so-called uncivilized societies, is built upon the precepts of the Bible. The concepts of love, respect, obedience, forgiveness, mercy and justice are all ultimately rooted in the Bible. You may go to the most depraved and uncivilized societies on the planet and you will find a moral code based upon the foundational teachings of the Bible. The fact that its principles existed ages before it was written testifies to the eternal nature of its ultimate Author, the God of all creation. His servant Peter testifies, "We have also a more sure word of prophecy; whereunto ye do well that ye take heed, as unto a light that shineth in a dark place, until the day dawn, and the day star arise in your hearts: Knowing this first, that no prophecy of the scripture is of any private interpretation. For the prophecy came not in old time by the will of man: but holy men of God spake as they were moved by the Holy Ghost" (2 peter 1:19-21).

The Bible's doctrines of morality and decency are as relevant today as they were in Eden. Failure to follow those precepts always lead to moral decay, social degradation, and ultimately destruction and death. Take a look at contemporary society and you will discover what it means to live outside God's moral standards as established in the Bible.

(3) **The Testimony of Science:** All true science is in perfect harmony with the Bible. Despite modern man's attempt to separate science from true religion, which is found only in the Bible, the evidence points unequivocally to the contrary. Many scientists of renown have been Bible believing Christians or Sabbath keeping Jews. Sir Isaac Newton, Francis Bacon, Louis Pasteur, Albert Einstein, to name a few, were all God-fearing men. Their contributions to science, which benefit us all, are undeniable.

Long before so called modern 'science' confirmed that the earth was round, Isaiah declared, "It is He (God) who sitteth upon the circle of the earth" (Isaiah 40:22). Job had long established what the scientists later confirmed. He proclaimed, "He (God) stretcheth out the north over the empty place, and hangeth the earth upon nothing" (Job 26:7). Modern scientific research into the origins of the universe are moving closer and closer to the Biblical account. They recognize the fact that the universe and its order of operation undeniably points to an intelligent designer who skillfully puts and holds everything together. It takes a great designer to design something as massive, complicated and orderly as the universe. The intricacies of the minutest atom demands that an intelligent designer must have been involved. He is Creator God.

(4) **The Testimony of History:** The events, places and personalities of the Bible, confirmed by historical facts, are today taken for granted. Take for example,

world history as foretold by the prophet Daniel in the 2nd, 7th, 8th & 11th chapters of his book. In it, Daniel delineated the nations, from his time in Babylon, to the current day and beyond. His predications are now proven historical fact. The world reign of Babylon followed by that of Media Persia, which was succeeded by Greece under Alexander the Great, then the rise of the Imperial Roman Empire, and its transformation to Papal Rome are all now a matter of proven history. The record of other great empires such as Egypt and Assyria testify to the accurate historicity of the Bible.

(5) **The Testimony of Prophecy:** Prophecy is history foretold. Therefore the only test of true prophecy is that it must come to pass. Of all the other so called religious books, none presents the element of foretelling history with an accompanying undeniable fulfillment. And, of all the prophecies in the Bible, none are more astounding than the prophecies concerning our Lord and Savior, Jesus Christ. The prophet Micah prophesied the exact place of His birth. (Micah 5:2) Isaiah foretold of His virgin birth (Isaiah 7:14). Zechariah told, hundreds of years before the event happened that the Savior will be sold for thirty pieces of silver (Zechariah 11:12,13). The prophet Daniel spoke before time of the exact length of Jesus' public ministry (Daniel 9:24-27). The Psalmist David assured us that His bones will not be broken; but that men would gamble for His garments (Psalm 22:16-18).

Those are but a few of hundreds of prophesies about the Messiah, Jesus Christ. Everyone, with the exception of His second coming, have come to pass just as the Bible predicted. They were all fulfilled with uncanny accuracy and divine precision. Isaiah writes on behalf of God, "I am the Lord...new things I declare before they spring forth I tell you of them" (Isaiah 42:8,9).

No so-called holy man or philosophical writer can truthfully utter those words. No other religious book can claim such credits. In fact, an examination of major religious writings outside the Bible would prove that the element of credible prophecy is woefully non-existent. Only a God who knows the future can predict the future and allow it come to pass.

(5) **The Testimony of Archaeology:** There has never been an archaeological find in the Bible lands that contradicted the historical record of the Bible. Quite the contrary, those finds confirm exactly what the Bible records. Critics have repeatedly been proven wrong as new discoveries confirm Biblical people, places, and events. Classical case in point is the Dead Sea Scrolls discovered in 1947. The discoveries of ancient writings by a Bedouin goat herder proved to be in remarkable conformity with facts and events mentioned in the Bible. Part of the find was a precise, original rendering of the book of Isaiah as we know it today.

Another remarkable archaeological find is that of the discovery Abraham's home, the city of Ur, by Sir

Leonard Woolley in 1936. His discoveries confirmed the existence and customs of Patriarchal times, as described in the Bible. The Bible record is endorsed by archaeological finds at such places as Ur, Mari, Boghazkoi, and Nineveh. The discoveries of written records in these areas prove that they were written from that day—not just put down in writing many centuries later. They bear the marks of eyewitness reporting.

(7) **The Testimony of a Changed Life:** The greatest testimony to the authenticity and divine nature of the Bible is its power to transform the life of both the believer and the non-believer alike. Many are familiar with that most enduring hymn, Amazing Grace. Few, however, know of the life changing experience of its author that led him to pen those amazing words.

John Newton was engaged in the most ignominious of human endeavors, the African slave trade. On one of his trips from West Africa to England, he heard a preacher spoke the message of salvation. John Newton was so moved that he obtained a Bible, which he took with him on his voyage back to Africa. On one moonlit night, he came above deck. Intrigued by the awesomeness of God, revealed in the starry heavens as it blanketed the endless expanse of the majestic ocean, he retired to his cabin and penned the words of that now redeeming hymn, Amazing Grace.

This writer's story is a living testimony. The word reached him in a life of riotous living characterized by drugs, alcohol, gambling, thievery and licentiousness. It brought him to a life of devotion to God and dedication to work of the ministry of Jesus Christ. The apostle Paul, in his usually forceful fashion, proclaims, "Therefore if any man be in Christ, he is a new creature: old things are passed away; behold, all things are become new" (2 Corinthians 5:17). This writer is a living testimony to that fact.

Ellen G. White, the renowned 19th century Bible Commentator, who the Smithsonian Magazine cites as one of the ten most influential religious leaders of all time, offers this insightful commentary: 'The Word of God, like the character of its divine Author, presents mysteries that can never be fully comprehended by finite beings. If it were possible for created beings to attain to a full understanding of God and His works, then, having reached this point, there would be for them no further discovery of truth, no growth in knowledge, no further development of mind or heart. God would no longer be supreme; and men, having reached the limit of knowledge and attainment, would cease to advance. Let us thank God that it is not so. God is infinite; in Him are "all the treasures of wisdom and knowledge" (Colossians 2:3).

In the natural world we are constantly surrounded with mysteries that we cannot fathom…. Should we then be surprised to find that in the spiritual world also there are mysteries that we cannot fathom? The mysteries of the Bible are among the strongest evidences of its divine inspiration. If it contained no account of God but that which we could comprehend; if His greatness and majesty could be grasped by finite minds, then the Bible would not, as now, bear the unmistakable evidences of divinity.

The more we search the Bible, the deeper is our conviction that it is the word of the living God, and human reason bows before the majesty of divine revelation. Christ will lead the redeemed ones beside the river of life and will open to them that which while on this earth they could not understand. In the light that shines from the throne, mysteries will disappear, and the soul will be filled with astonishment at the simplicity of the things that were never before comprehended'. (The Faith We Live By, pg. 14, E.G. White).

The Bible is truly the Only Sure Foundation. It is the autobiographical record of the One who died for you.

Chapter 12

HAVING FAITH IN THE FOUNDATION

*T*here is no other book like the Bible. In a class all by itself, this all time, best-selling masterpiece contains the sustenance that every hungering soul desires. Sadly, many are dying of hunger and of thirst because they refuse partake of the bounty that it offers.

One respected Bible commentator describes it this way: "The Bible unfolds truth with a simplicity and a perfect adaptation to the needs and longings of the human heart that has astonished and charmed the most highly cultivated minds, while it enables the humblest and uncultured to discern the way of salvation. And yet these simply stated truths lay hold upon subjects so elevated, so far-reaching, so infinitely beyond the power of human comprehension, that we can accept them only because God has declared them" (Steps to Christ, pg. 107, E. G. White). This being the case, it's surprising to find out the low level of regard that so many, including many who call themselves Christians, have for the Holy Bible.

An article in a recent Christian Online magazine noted: "More Americans now believe that the Bible is a book of fables and history than those who believe it's the literal Word of God, a Gallup poll has found. Even fewer than a third of Christians say it's to be taken literally". The article continued, "Over the past three decades, Americans' view of the Bible as the literal Word of God has been declining, while their view that the Bible is a collection of fables, myths and history recorded by man has been increasing."

Among all sampled Americans, over 1,100 in number, fewer than one in four, or 24 percent in total, said the Bible is "the actual Word of God, and is to be taken literally, word for word. A slightly higher 26 percent said that the Bible is "a book of fables, legends, history and moral precepts recorded by man. While another 47 percent said they believe the Bible is "inspired by God, not all to be taken literally."

Further, the article stated, "Belief in the Bible as the literal Word of God was lowest among young adults aged 18 to 29-year-olds, with 12 percent supporting such a view, and highest among the 50 to 64 year-olds, at 31 percent. College graduate students were also less likely than those with some college and those with no college to take the Bible literally.

Americans are more accepting of immorality than ever before, the Gallup poll found. The country may already be seeing this in growing public acceptance of a variety of behaviors that were once largely frowned on from a Christian perspective — ranging from gay marriage and premarital sex to out-of-wedlock births and physician-assisted suicide. While 1 in 5 Americans read the entire Bible, most call it a good source of morals.

"Americans in all age groups still largely accept the Bible as a Holy document, but most of these downplay God's direct role in it. That could mean people are more willing than in the past to believe it is open to interpretation — if man, not God, wrote the Bible, more can be questioned", Gallup analyzed. "And that, in turn, may have consequences for where Americans come down on a number of morally tinged issues" (Christian Post, May 16, 2017).

In another survey by the Pew Research Center, an organization which follows and reports on religious and other cultural trends, it was reported that more than 78% of mainline Protestants believe that humans have evolved over time. What's more puzzling about this report is that a significant number of those who hold this belief also believe that a supreme being guided this evolutionary process. In plain language, this means that more than ¾ of people who call themselves Christians do not believe in the Bible record of creation. Not believing in the Biblical creation leads to gross deception about Jesus Christ and the story of human redemption. For if you do not believe in the creation, how can you believe in, or seek, redemption? Redemption from what?

And this is exactly what we have in Christendom today. Rather than the Story of Redemption, with Jesus' sacrifice as the foundation being preached, church attendees are served with a plethora of what the apostle Paul calls another Gospel (Galatians 1:8). In the place of proclaiming man's sinful nature and his need of a Savior, Christians are told how good they are and how better they can become by following the latest 5-point strategy to success. Congregants are fed with a dazzling dose of intellectual philosophy by charismatic, motivational speakers whose purpose is to entertain, amass fame and fortune, rather than lift up Jesus of Nazareth, the only Savior of the world. Replacing the word of God is mystical meditations designed to bring the people into 'closer touch' with themselves. Worldly entertainment mixed with feel-good theology has supplanted the precious Hymns of Zion under the cover of 'Praise and Worship'. Faith in the Bible is almost totally eradicated. Simple faith in God's word is no longer encouraged.

Despite all this, we can and must trust the Bible as God's inspired word and have faith in it as the only foundation on which to build our Christian experience. The apostle Paul teaches us, "For whatsoever things were written aforetime were written for our learning, that we through patience and comfort of the scriptures might have hope" (Romans 15:4). He continues, "So then faith cometh by hearing, and hearing by the word of God" (Romans 10:17). Jesus pleads, "And why call ye Me, Lord, Lord, and do not the things which I say? Whosoever cometh to me, and heareth my sayings, and doeth them, I will shew you to whom he is like: He is like a man which built an house, and digged deep, and laid the foundation on a rock: and when the flood arose, the stream beat vehemently upon that house, and could not shake it: for it was founded upon a rock. But he that heareth, and doeth not, is like a man that without a foundation built an house upon the earth; against which the stream did beat vehemently, and immediately it fell; and the ruin of that house was great" (Luke 6:46-49).

In the world today, we are witnessing Christianity manifesting itself in various forms. Many are sincere about what they believe, say, and do; but sincere belief in error will not save us. Drinking a glass of cool aid mixed with cyanide will surely kill you whether you sincerely believe it is poison or not.

We see the rise of Greek Intellectual Philosophy in our churches, seminaries and Christian schools where scholarly knowledge and higher critical criticism supplants 'A thus saith the Lord'. So-called ministers are no longer pastors who serve the saints and seek to lead them to Jesus Christ. Rather, they strive to become Dr. So and So, in order that the saints can look up to them as someone of a higher order.

The Christian church has long ago been imbued with pagan mythology in the form of mother/son worship and Sunday sacredness along with a myriad of other beliefs and doctrines which cannot be found in the Bible. Currently, we are witnessing the rapid advancement into Eastern Mysticism. This Emerging Church movement advances Contemplative Prayer, Centering Prayer, and a plethora of feel-good delusions. One's personal feelings becomes superior to the word of God. Instead of calling for a separation from the world as Jesus demands, we hear the call to let us come together with the world on common ground.

The popular opinion is that fundamentally, we're all serving the same God. Therefore, as Christians, Jews, Hindus, Buddhists, Evangelicals, Catholics, Muslims, New Agers, and everybody else, we can all come together in the name of world peace. But Jesus, the Prince of peace, says, "Think not that I am come to send peace on earth: I came not to send peace, but a sword. For I am come to set a man at variance against his father, and the daughter against her mother, and the daughter in law against her mother in law. And a man's foes shall be they of his own household. He that loveth father or mother more than me is not worthy of me: and he that loveth son or daughter more than me is not worthy of me" (Matthew 10:34-37).

Who can deny our own American homegrown form of Christianity in the form of the Prosperity Gospel with its Name-it/Claim-it dose of heretical poison and self-actualization theology? Then there is the increasing promulgation of the Social Gospel, which is nothing less than a rapid move towards Marxist Socialism with the union of church and state. All these of course are advanced in the name of Jesus Christ. Nevertheless, the Bible's clear teaching that salvation is obtainable only by God's grace, through faith in His Son and our Savior, Jesus Christ, is woefully missing. So often, a Bible is absent from the presenter's possession. In the rear cases that they are seen, they are seldom or never opened.

Now, all these popular sentiments sound very good on the surface and some of them may have a bit of truth and in them. But something is missing, sorely missing, that is the power of Gospel to transform the life from sin to righteousness. Putting away of sin from our lives has become a forgotten notion of the ancient past. Honestly, without that all else is meaningless. That is what is lacking from all the manifestations of Christianity mentioned earlier. The truth about Calvary is abandoned. Without it, our Christianity is in vain. The apostle Paul makes it very plain in his letter to the Corinthian believers. He says, "And if Christ be not risen, then is our preaching in vain, and your faith in vain...And if Christ be not raised, your faith is in vain; ye are yet in your sins" (1 Corinthians 15:14,17).

Too often so-called Christian leaders bypass Calvary and turn the spotlight on themselves...look who I am...look at how many are following me...look how many degrees, mansions, and luxury vehicles I have.

They deceitfully avoid sharing or are willingly ignorant of the fact that Jesus is interceding as our Heavenly High Priest and is getting ready to come and take us home to spend eternity with Him.

Few shares that the cross of Calvary is not at all about living an earthly prosperous life; but rather the transformation of our characters to be like Jesus. Hence, Jesus declares in the most famous and powerful sermon ever preached, called the Sermon on the Mount: "Not everyone that saith unto me, Lord, Lord, shall enter into the kingdom of heaven; but he that doeth the will of my Father which is in heaven. Many will say to me in that day, Lord, Lord, have we not prophesied in thy name? and in thy name have cast out devils? and in thy name done many wonderful works? And then will I profess unto them, I never knew you: depart from me, ye that work iniquity" (Matthew 7:21-23). These are perhaps the most solemn words in all Holy Writ.

But how can we be assured that we are not in that company? How can we be certain that we do have it right? There is only one way and one way only...that is trusting, having faith in God's word, the Holy Bible, the Only True Foundation.

The prophet Isaiah declared, "To the law and to the testimony: if they speak not according to this word, it is because there is no light in them." (Isaiah 8:20). The people of God are directed to the Scriptures as their safeguard against the influence of false teachers and the delusive power of spirits of darkness. Satan employs every possible device to prevent men from obtaining a knowledge of the Bible; for its plain utterances reveal his deceptions.

At every revival of God's work the prince of evil is aroused to more intense activity; he is now putting forth his utmost efforts for a final struggle against Christ and His followers. The last great delusion is soon to open before us. Antichrist is to perform his marvelous works in our sight. So closely will the counterfeit resemble the true that it will be impossible to distinguish between them except by the Holy Scriptures.

By their testimony every statement and every miracle must be tested. Those who endeavor to obey all the commandments of God will be opposed and derided. They can stand only in God. In order to endure the trial before them, they must understand the will of God as revealed in His word; they can honor Him only as they have a right conception of His character, government, and purposes, and act in accordance with them. None but those who have fortified the mind with the truths of the Bible will stand through the last great conflict. To every soul will come the searching test: Shall I obey God rather than men? The decisive hour is even now at hand. Are our feet planted on the rock of God's immutable word? Are we prepared to stand firm in defense of the commandments of God and the faith of Jesus? (E.G White, Great Controversy, pg. 593).

Everything we do, whatever we believe in this Christian life is based on faith; even accepting the Bible for what it says it is, the word of God, is based on faith. The very first words of the Bible are, "In the beginning, God created the heaven and the earth" (Genesis 1:1). Do you believe those words? If you do, then you must believe everything else that follows. Since none of us were there when God created the world, then it stands to reason that it is only by faith we can believe, not only the creation story, but the Bible as a whole. Those first words of the Bible demand unquestioning faith in God. He gave us no preamble. No theological exegesis is put forth. No intellectual philosophy is engaged in. God simply, but quite assuredly and unapologetically declared "He Created". To believe the Bible requires faith. Being a Christian requires faith in the Only Sure Foundation.

But what is this thing called faith? Do we really understand what it entails? The apostle Paul gives us the classical definition: "Now faith is the substance of things hoped for, the evidence of things not seen" (Hebrews 11:1). Simply put, faith means trusting and believing in that which you cannot experience with the natural senses. Faith is a spiritual concept that emanates from an infinite God to finite man. From a Biblical perspective, faith is trusting God and accepting what He says in His word as fact, yea verily as reality. Faith means that God will bring to pass in your life that which He has promised. It demands believing all that God has revealed in His word, the holy Bible, about Himself.

Thus Paul continues, "But without faith, it is impossible to please God: for he that cometh to God must believe that He is, and that He is a rewarder of them that diligently seek Him" (Hebrews 11:6).

Contrary to popular belief, particularly among some Christian circles, faith is not mind power. It is not the ability to visualize one's personal desires, and through the power of the mind, bring them to pass. Such a concept, though appealing to the carnal nature, is false and dangerous. Faith is not name it and claim it. Rather, it is trusting God that whatever He allows to come to pass in your life is for your good. Paul again admonishes us, "And we know that all things work together for good to them that love God, to them that are the called according to His purposes" (Romans 8:28).

The patriarch Abraham understood clearly the nature of faith. When called upon by God to leave his kinsfolk and go to a place wither he knew not of, Abraham willingly obeyed. When told by God that he would have a child in his old age, though he did not believe initially; Abraham finally trusted God to bring to pass in his life that which God had promised. Later, when asked by God to sacrifice the son of his old age, the very son that God had promised and fulfilled, Abraham, without any hesitation, obeyed. Moses therefore talks of Abraham: "And he (Abraham) believed in the Lord; and He (God) counted it to him for righteousness" (Genesis15:6). The apostle Paul writes to the believers at

Galatia: "Know ye therefore that they which are of faith, the same are the children of Abraham" (Galatians 3:7).

The patriarch Job, in like fashion, demonstrated his faith in God. The story of Job is quite familiar. It is from this narrative that the phrase 'you have faith like Job' is derived. Job was very rich and prosperous. He was a faithful servant of Creator God and was considered blameless in the eyes of his Creator. The devil, the enemy of our souls, approached God and asked Him for permission to take Job's family and all his earthly belongings. The devil thought that Job would refrain from serving God if his material wealth was taken away. God granted the devil his wishes. But Job remained faithful to God. In the depths of his deprivation and misery, characterized by abject poverty, a body of bones covered only with skin emaciated with putrefying sores, Job exclaimed, "Though He slay me, yet will I trust in Him" (Job 12:15). That's faith. It is believing God and trusting in His promises, regardless of your financial, physical or social condition.

Talking about the heroes of faith, the apostle Paul assures us, "These all died in faith, not having received the promises, but having seen them a for off, and were persuaded of them, and embraced them, and confessed that they were strangers and pilgrims on the earth...And these all, having obtained a good report through faith, received not the promise: God having provided some better thing for us, that they without us should not be made perfect" (Hebrews 11:13, 39-40). What a solemn thought!! Therefore, today, more than ever, the Christian's faith must be similarly rooted and grounded.

But how do we get this faith? Paul answers, "For whatsoever things were written aforetime were written for our learning, that we through patience and comfort of the Scriptures might have hope" (Romans 15:4). The learned apostle also tells us, "The Just shall by faith" (Romans 1:17). Faith ultimately is simply believing what God says in His word, the Only Sure Foundation, and acting in accordance with it.

Jesus asks the question, "When the Son of Man cometh, will He find faith on earth?" (Luke 18:8). The faith He is referring to is verily the faith He requires us to have in His word, the Holy Bible. It is the Only Sure Foundation.

As you examine the Bible, you'll discover that in the very act of reading it your faith will be strengthened. Consequently, you will conclude that it is indeed the Only True Foundation and that you can have faith in it. And surely, Jesus, the One who died for you will find faith on earth when He comes.

Chapter 13

WHAT HE REQUIRES OF US

*H*ow often have you heard that since we are Christians, we do not have to keep God's law? 'That was just for the Jews,' many claim. But how accurate is that claim? Is this assertion substantiated by the Only Sure Foundation, the Holy Bible?

The word 'Law' denotes a legal concept. It is a principle which suggests that someone, in a superior position, puts forth certain rules and regulations, which another, in an inferior position, is bound to follow. If those rules and regulations are violated, then the law provides for certain consequences or punishments. Law is a universal concept. It is the foundation of all human endeavors. All our affairs in this life are conducted based on law. All things, animate and inanimate, are governed by law. From the tiniest atom to the mightiest star, law is the basis of their existence.

In our homes there are laws. There are rules established by our local governments. Then there are state laws. Here in the United States of America, as in all other civilized countries, all citizens are obligated to abide by the supreme law of the land called the Constitution. All other laws of the land are subject to that law. The violation thereof can result in serious consequences that may affect the entire population.

No rational person would suggest that the laws governing our temporal lives or natural elements might be broken without suffering the consequences of their violation. Laws and consequences are the foundations of human experience. It has been that way from creation. It has continued so throughout the history of mankind and will remain thus as long as we exist.

Should we do away with, or otherwise eradicate those laws, the result would be chaotic. Now those are only man-made laws. It follows, therefore, that the God of the universe must also have laws by which the galaxies, planets and stars in the heavens must abide. Likewise, His greatest creation, mankind, must be bound by His laws. How much more serious then, can be the consequences, for the violation of God's laws? With respect to humanity, the violation of God's law is called sin. The consequence of which is death.

The law laid down by our Creator to the first humans was this, "Of every tree of the garden thou mayest freely eat: But of the tree of the knowledge of good and evil, thou shalt not eat of it: for in the day that thou eatest thereof thou shalt surely die" (Genesis 2:16-17). The apostle Paul reaffirms what God told our first parents in the Garden of Eden. He writes, "The wages of sin is death" (Romans 6:23). And what is sin? It is what Adam and Eve did in the Garden of Eden, *i.e.* disobeying God's law. The apostle John makes it plain: "Whosoever commits sin, transgress (break) the law; for sin is the transgression of the law" (1 John 3:4). But which Law?

Of all the laws given to man by God, none is of higher value than the Ten Commandments. This law encompasses all other laws and forms the foundation of God's government. It is the supreme law by which God intends all men to live. It is God's Constitution. The Psalmist David characterizes it thus, "I have seen an end of all perfection: but thy commandment is exceeding broad" (Psalm 119:96). That law, God's Constitution, was codified and delivered by Creator God to His servant Moses.

It reads:

(**1**) Thou shall have no other god before Me.

(**2**) Thou shall not make unto thee any graven image of any likeness of anything that is in heaven above, or that is in the earth beneath, or that is in the water under the earth: thou shall not bow down thyself to them, nor serve them: for I the Lord thy God am a jealous God visiting the iniquity of the fathers upon the children unto the third and fourth generation of them that hate me and showing mercy unto thousands of them love me and keep my commandments.

(**3**) Thou shall not take the name of the Lord thy God in vain; for the Lord will not hold him guiltless that take His name in vain.

(**4**) Remember the Sabbath day to keep it holy. Six days shall thou labor, and do all thy work: but the seventh day is the Sabbath of the Lord Thy God: in it thou shall not do any work: thou nor thy son, nor thy daughter, nor thy manservant, nor thy maidservant, nor thy cattle, nor thy stranger that is within thy gates. For in six days The Lord made heaven and earth, the sea and all that in them is, and rested on the seventh day: wherefore the Lord blessed the seventh day and hallowed it.

(**5**) Honor thy father and thy mother: that thy days may be long upon the land, which the Lord, thy God giveth thee.

(**6**)Thou shall not kill.

(**7**)Thou shall not commit adultery.

(**8**)Thou shall not steal.

(**9**) Thou shall not bear false witness against thy neighbor.

(**10**) Thou shall not covet thy neighbor's house. Thou shall not covet thy neighbor's wife: nor his manservant, nor his maidservant, nor his ox, nor his ass, nor anything that is thy neighbor's (Exodus 20:3-17).

Of such importance is God's Ten Commandment law that He trusted no one to write them down. Lest there be any misunderstanding or misinterpretation, the Scripture records that God wrote them on tables of stone with His own finger. His servant records, "And He gave unto Moses, when He had made an end of communing with him upon mount Sinai, two tables of testimony, tables of stone, written with the finger of God" (Exodus 31:18).

I thank God that nowhere in His word do we find Him annulling any part of his law. I praise Him even more for grace. Paul concludes, "But the gift of God is eternal life through Christ Jesus, our Lord" (Romans 6:23). Here Paul presents the antidote for breaking God's law and suffering the consequences thereof. That's grace--Jesus Christ paying the penalty for our transgressions. Paul explains, "But God commendeth his love toward us, in that, while we were yet sinners, Christ died for us" (Romans 5:8).

Clearly, Paul is not giving permission to sin because of God's grace to us, through Our Lord and Savior Jesus Christ. Rather, he is pointing us to keep the law, by the grace of God, and because of our love for Him. As Christians, our determination should be not to break any one of God's commandments. However, because of our fallen human nature, we do from time to time, succumb to temptation and sin. But, thanks to God for grace. Because of that grace so freely and abundantly given to us, we should strive to reflect the character of God. His character is exemplified by His holy law, the Ten Commandments. The apostle Paul reminds us,

"Moreover the law entered, that the offence might abound. But where sin abounded, grace did much more abound" (Romans 5:20). But then he cautions us, "Do we then make void the law through faith? God forbid: yea, we establish the law" (Romans 3:31). As Christians, we are called to a higher standard of accountability.

The apostle John presents true grace to us. He counsels, "If we confess our sins, he is faithful and just to forgive us our sins, and to cleanse us from all unrighteousness" (1 John 1:9). Then he reiterates, "My little children, these things write I unto you, that ye sin not. And if any man sin, we have an Advocate with the Father, Jesus Christ the Righteous. And He is the propitiation for our sins: and not for our sins only, but also for the sins of the whole world" (1 John 2: 1,2).

Being saved by grace means the turning away from sin and walking in righteousness. It means stop breaking God's law and start obeying it. We can., and must, obey God's law, by the power of the indwelling of the Holy Spirit, coupled with a willing and submissive heart.

Perhaps, the most misunderstood and misused passage of Scripture that is cited to show that God's law is abolished is this: "For sin shall not have dominion over you: for ye are not under the law, but under grace" (Romans 6:14). Too often, the very next verse is forgotten. Paul continued, "What then? Shall we sin (break the law) because we are not under the law, but under grace? God forbid" (Romans 6:15). Paul rhetorically asks the same question again, "what shall we say then? Shall we continue in sin (continue to break the law), that grace may abound? (Romans 6:1). The answer is the same—no we do not. Nowhere does Paul give license to break God's law because of grace. The law, to which Paul is referring, in each of these cases, is the Ten Commandment law. He is most assuredly pointing out that God's grace is both pardon from breaking His law and power to keep it.

A correct understanding of what grace is, and how Paul relates it to the law is necessary for properly comprehending what Paul is talking about. Here is an explanation. Biblical grace is a divine endowment bestowed by a Holy God upon sinful man. It is greater than all our sins. It is freely and abundantly lavished upon every member of the human family. Grace affords us pardon from our sins. It further empowers us to live without sin. It saves us from the condemnation of sin, which is death. It is that which God gives to us that we may have a chance to return to Him. Divine grace is not a license to break God's law. It is, indeed, the power to keep us from breaking the law, which is sin. It is a gift given by a Loving God to undeserving man. Grace is the divine influence upon the heart, drawing sinful man ever closer to his Holy Creator. Jesus declared to the woman, caught in adultery, who was about to suffer the consequences of her sin, "Neither do I condemn thee: go and sin no more" (John 8:11). This is the epitome of grace...amazing grace.

Jesus Christ, our Lord and Savior, came, died and lives that we may be restored to our Edenic image, a life of perfect obedience to His law. The angel assured Joseph, "And she shall bring forth a son, and thou shalt call his name Jesus: for He shall save his people from their sins (Matthew 1:21). Jesus' last prayer for us, before He proceeded to pay the price for our sins, is this, "That they all may be one; as thou, Father, art in me, and I in thee, that they also may be one in us: that the world may believe that thou hast sent me. And the glory which thou gavest me I have given them; that they may be one, even as we are one: I in them, and thou in me, that they may be made perfect in one; and that the world may know that thou hast sent me, and hast loved them, as thou hast loved me" (John 17:21-23).

To those who profess that God's grace does away with His law, I ask a simple question: 'how can we be one with Jesus and His father if we dispose of His law?' The wise man Solomon plainly presents that which God requires of us. He declares, "Let us hear the conclusion of the whole matter: Fear God and keep his commandments: for this is the whole duty of man" (Ecclesiastes 12:13). Jesus Christ, our Creator, Redeemer and Lawgiver, is the only example we should follow. He kept the law perfectly. We must always endeavor to do likewise. By His grace we can. He pleads with us, "If ye love me, keep my commandments" (John 14:15).

That's what He, the One wo died for you, requires of us.

Chapter 14

OUR PERFECT EXAMPLE

The work of a prophet has always been to correct God's people and point them towards God. Also, their work involved comforting and consoling God's people when they are hurt and confirming their actions when they are on the right path. Not only were they teachers by expounding upon the word of God; but their lifestyles testified to their connection with God. At all times, during their ministry, prophets lived according to the word and will of God. Above all, a prophet serves as the mouthpiece of God. No one fulfilled such a mission more than our Lord and Savior, Jesus Christ. He thus spoke of Himself, "The Spirit of the Lord is upon me, because the Lord hath anointed Me to preach the gospel to the poor, He hath sent Me to heal the broken-hearted, to preach deliverance to the captives and recovering of sight to the blind, to set at liberty them that are bruised" (Luke 4:18).

Quite interestingly, it was on the Sabbath-day that Jesus made that declaration, thus revealing to the world who He truly was and what His mission was all about.

Such are the blessings of the Sabbath. The record reveals, "And He (Jesus) came to Nazareth, where He had been brought up; and, as His custom was, He went into the synagogue on the Sabbath-day, and stood up for to read" (Luke 4:16).

This record alone is evidence enough regarding Jesus' attitude towards God's Sabbath. How men can conjecture that Jesus abolished His Sabbath is beyond reason and without Scriptural foundation.

The Scripture confirms that Jesus was a prophet. Moses prophesied, "The Lord thy God will rise up unto thee a prophet from the midst of thee, of thy brethren, like unto me; unto Him ye shall hearken" (Deuteronomy 18:15). Lest there be any misunderstanding as to who that prophet would be, the Evangelist Stephen, as he was being stoned to death by the leaders who rejected Jesus, proclaimed, "This is that Moses, which said unto the children of Israel, a prophet shall the Lord thy God raise up unto you of your brethren, like unto me, Him ye shall hear" (Acts 7:37).

The apostle John concurs. In referring to Jesus, he declared, "Many of the people therefore when they heard this saying, said, of a truth this is "THE PROPHET" (John 7:40).

Jesus was not just that Prophet. The apostle Peter declares that He is our Perfect Example. Says he, "For even hereunto were ye called, because Christ also suffered for us, leaving us an example that we should follow His steps" (1 Peter 2:21). As we follow Jesus, through the dusty streets of Palestine, we will surely discover what He has left us as an example with regards to God's Sabbath. It, like all His revelations to us, are matters of faith.

He, being his/her Perfect Example, the committed Christian should do likewise by honoring God on His holy and blessed Sabbath-day. By so doing, they would indeed be in the company of their Savior thus revealing to the world their saving relationship with Him.

As we look unto Jesus, the Author and Finisher of our faith, we observe that He, above all men, kept the Sabbath in highest regard. He did not, as some teach, break the Sabbath. Had He done so, He would be just like us, lost sinners. Consequently, He could in no wise have been our Savior. Ultimately, it is to Him that we look as we seek to understand and settle this issue of God's Sabbath in our hearts.

Beyond our first encounter with Jesus on the Sabbath-day when He revealed Himself to the world, we find the account of Jesus and His disciples being accused by the Pharisees of breaking the Sabbath. Matthew reports, "At that time, Jesus went on the Sabbath day through the corn; and His disciples were an hungered, and began to pluck the ears of corn and to eat...But when the Pharisees saw it, they said unto Him, 'Behold thy disciples do that which is not lawful to do upon the Sabbath day'" (Matthew 12:1,2).

In responding to their charge, Jesus reminded them of David and his men when they entered the sanctuary and ate the shewbread, which was not 'lawful' for them to do. Jesus also reminded them of certain indiscretions of the ancient priests in carrying out their duties. His (Jesus) conclusion to the matter is recorded thus, "But if ye had known what this means, I will have mercy and not sacrifice, ye would not have condemned the guiltless...For the Son of man is Lord even of the Sabbath day" (Matthew 12:7,8).

First, Jesus was not the one who plucked the ears of corn. The Scripture is abundantly clear that it was his disciples. Secondly, Jesus declared them to be guiltless. For one to obtain food and eat on the Sabbath-day, if they are hungry, is not breaking the Sabbath. It is clear from the account, in three Gospels, that Jesus and His disciples did not purposely go out on the Sabbath-day to pick corn in defiance of the commandment not to do any work on the Sabbath-day.

In fact, it is obvious that they were in transit from one location to another. During that time, Jesus' disciples got hungry and proceeded to feed themselves. More importantly, Jesus used the occasion to expose the hypocrisy of the Pharisees in their exacting, non-Biblical rules regarding the Sabbath. Had His disciples been wrong in their actions, Jesus would have been the first to rebuke them. He did so, on other occasions, when they erred in His presence. Please note also that even if His disciples had erred, Jesus did not condemn them, but rather, extended grace and mercy. That's a good thing to do on the Sabbath-day.

Forgiveness for breaking the law is not the same as condoning one's breaking the law. Finally, and most importantly, Jesus declared that He is Lord of the Sabbath. Nowhere in this episode did Jesus make the slightest reference to doing away with the Sabbath. He simply reinforced the principle that the Sabbath was still binding. The Savior further taught that He would forgive men if, in ignorance, they transgress the Sabbath or any other commandment.

As we follow Jesus, we find Him in the temple on yet another Sabbath-day. The example is again given that attending worship services on the Sabbath-day is what God requires of us. By the example of Jesus, and not the tradition of men, we must order our lives. In doing His work of mercy for which He came, Jesus was accused of breaking the Sabbath. The record reads, "And it came to pass also on another Sabbath, that He entered into the synagogue and taught, and there was a man whose right hand was withered. And the Scribes and the Pharisees watched him, whether He would heal on the Sabbath-day; that they may find an accusation against Him" (Luke 6:6,7).

Jesus, perceiving their thoughts, posed the questions, "What man shall there be among you that shall have one sheep, and if it fall into a pit on the Sabbath-day, will he not lay hold on it and lift it out?

How much then is a man better than a sheep? Wherefore is it lawful to do well on the Sabbath days" (Matthew 12:11-12).

Of course, the Scribes and Pharisees were dumbfounded and could not answer Him truthfully. If they did, they would have condemned themselves. They therefore kept their silence. Then Jesus, looking upon the man with the withered hand, declared, "Stretch forth thy hand." (Matthew 12:13). And Jesus healed him. Again, nowhere in this account, did Jesus remotely indicate that the Sabbath was no longer in effect. He certainly did not indicate that it was in any way less binding upon men because He came. Quite to the contrary, He confirmed that not only is the Sabbath-day yet holy; but showed by example that it is lawful, in the eyes of God, to perform acts of mercy on the Sabbath day.

Accompanying Jesus, again on the Sabbath-day, we remain with Him as He makes His way to church. On His way there, He encountered a crippled man. This man found it impossible to get others to help him step into the pool of Bethesda. It was the prevailing belief that if, at certain times, one steps into the pool, he would be healed. Jesus, upon seeing this man and the helpless condition in which he found himself, was moved with compassion. Jesus appealed to him, "Wilt thou be made whole?" (John 5:7). The crippled man, obviously not realizing who it was that spoke to him, replied by recounting all the problems he was having in getting healed. To which Jesus responded, "Rise, take up thy bed and walk" (John 5:8).

Again, because it was on the Sabbath-day, the Jewish leaders were extremely indignant with Jesus and sought to persecute and slander Him. They pursued Him relentlessly until they finally caught up with Him. Realizing their motives and reading the intents of their hearts, Jesus asked, "Did not Moses give you the law, and yet none of you keep the law...I have done one work and ye all marveled... Moses therefore gave unto you circumcision (not because it is of Moses, but of the fathers) and ye on the Sabbath-day receive circumcision, that the Law of Moses should not be broken; are ye angry at me, because I have made a man every whit whole on the Sabbath-day...Judge not according to the appearance, but judge righteous judgment" (John 7:19,21- 24). As usual, Jesus illustrated to them and to us today, that it is perfectly in harmony with God's will to relieve the burden of suffering humanity on the Sabbath-day.

We are once more faced with a situation where Sabbath keeping is confirmed and uplifted by Jesus. He taught, by both precept and example, what is proper to do on the Sabbath-day. Though many see these incidents as evidence not to keep God's Sabbath-day holy; Jesus, our Savior, plainly demonstrated differently.

These encounters exemplify that we are to keep the Sabbath-day holy according to God's command. They help us to do so by giving us the divine pattern of what it is permissible to do and is accepted by God on the Sabbath. Jesus teaches us that it is right in the sight of God to do good on the Sabbath-day. In stark contrast to what false prophets and teachers advocate, Jesus does not teach that men should profane or otherwise do away with the Sabbath-day, simply because He came and died for us. Instead, He gave us many examples of how to keep the Sabbath-day holy. If we claim Him as our Savior then we must follow His example.

As He gazed down the highway of prophetic time and foresaw the destruction of His beloved city, Jerusalem, and the end of the world, Jesus warned, "But pray ye that your flight be not in the winter, neither on the Sabbath-day" (Matthew 24:20). It was almost another forty years before the destruction of Jerusalem occurred. Here is the clearest indication that Jesus did not abolish the Sabbath. Rather, it plainly presents the fact that the Sabbath should be kept after His death, even to the end of time.

Jesus, not unlike the other prophets before and after Him, constantly kept the importance of God's true Sabbath before the eyes and minds of the people. He, the only true Messiah, demonstrated the sanctity of the Sabbath even in death. All four of the gospel writers, Matthew, Mark, Luke and John, testify to this fact. They all are remarkably consistent in reporting the events of Jesus' death, burial, and resurrection. This being the case, the mention of one such account will be sufficient to illustrate the point of Jesus' rest on the Sabbath, even in death.

Luke records thus, "And that day was the preparation day, and the Sabbath drew on... And the women also, which came with Him from Galilee, followed after, and beheld the sepulchre and how His body was laid...And they returned and prepared spices and ointments and rested the Sabbath day, according to the commandment" (Luke 23:54-56). Certainly, Jesus' disciples never gave any thought to the notion that because their Savior was crucified, the Sabbath was abolished. Nowhere, in His three and one half years of earthly ministry, did Jesus address the issue of changing or abolishing His Seventh-day Sabbath.

As He laid in the grave on the Sabbath-day, His disciples honored Him by continuing to follow what He had taught them by example. The sanctity of the Sabbath has never changed. We who claim to be followers of Jesus Christ must strive, by His grace, to do as He did, in all areas of our lives, including keeping of His Sabbath-day holy. The apostle John cautions us, "He that saith he abideth in Him, ought himself also to walk, even as He walked" (1 John 2:6). And how did Jesus walk regarding the Sabbath-day? He honored it and kept it holy according to the commandment. So, must we. In fact, he reminds us, "The Sabbath was made for man and not man for the Sabbath: Therefore the Son of man is Lord also of the Sabbath" (Mark 2:27-28).

In all the examples cited regarding Jesus Christ's attitude toward the Sabbath, we are presented with the facts of how He perceived the Sabbath and how He reflected it in His personal life. For the Jews of Jesus' time, the Sabbath was a burden. It was a time to be rigidly observed by trying to comply with a regimen of man-made rules, rituals and regulations. That which God has given as a blessing at creation, man had corrupted by blending with a multitude of unwarranted rites and unbiblical regulations, thus making it burdensome. Unfortunately, that's the legacy of the Sabbath that has been handed down through the ages. That is a false picture. By boldly defying human custom and tradition, Jesus has left us with the right picture and the perfect example of how to keep His Sabbath-day holy.

For Christians, God's Sabbath-day is a reminder of who is our Creator. It helps us to reflect upon our total dependence upon Him for our every need. God's Sabbath is also a commemoration of who is our Redeemer. Paul stresses to Titus, "Who (Jesus Christ) gave himself for us, that He might redeem us from all iniquity and purify unto himself a peculiar people, zealous of good work" (Titus 2:14). Paul additionally declared to the Jews who had come to accept Jesus as their Lord and Savior, "For He spoke in a certain place of the seventh-day on this wise, 'and God did rest on the seventh day from all His works... For if Jesus had given them rest, then would He not afterward have spoken of another day... There remaineth therefore a rest for the people of God" (Hebrews 4:4, 8-9).

Our rest is in Jesus Christ. Keeping His Sabbath-day holy is an outward demonstration of that rest in Him. It is an honor, a joy, and a privilege to do so. It is an act of love and obedience. Sabbath keeping is a revelation of God's love and compassion for all humanity. It is a blessing. It is truthfully abiding in Jesus. It is being yoked up with Him. To keep God's Sabbath-day holy is to delight in Jesus Christ as our Creator, Savior, and Redeemer. God's Sabbath-day is a sign to the world that we are truly His.

Jesus Christ, on His sojourn on this earth, taught us how to truly keep His Sabbath-day holy. He continues to empower us to do so today. He desires and empowers us to keep all His laws, including His blessed Sabbath-day. When we look unto Him as our example, we will come to realize that Sabbath keeping is not a mere round of rituals, encompassing a list of burdensome rules. Instead, we will experience being a partaker of a joyous experience in Him who is our Maker and Redeemer, the One who died for you.

If you, by faith, claim Him to be your Creator and accept Him as your Savior and Redeemer, then He simply asks you, "Remember His Sabbath day to keep it Holy". It is not a burdensome task that He had to abolish at Calvary. Keeping God's Sabbath holy is simply a love response to the one who created us, saves from the penalty of sin, is saving us from the power of sin, and will ultimately deliver us from the presence of sin from a world mangled with death and woe.

Our Lord and Savior emphatically declares, "Think not that I am come to destroy the law, or the prophets. I am not come to destroy, but to fulfill. For verily I say unto you, till heaven and earth pass, one jot or one tittle shall in no wise pass from the law, till all be fulfilled. Whosoever therefore break one of these least commandments, and shall teach men so, he shall be called the least in heaven: but whosoever shall do and teach them, the same shall be called great in the kingdom of heaven" (Matthew 5:17-19).

Jesus' fulfillment of the law was prophesied by the prophet Isaiah thus, "The Lord is well pleased for His righteousness' sake: He will magnify the law and make it honorable" (Isaiah 42:21). His fulfillment of the law is not to do away with it; but rather to make it clearer through His living example. He kept it perfectly as an example for us to follow. Jesus never asks us what we think about the law, or what does Paul say about it. He simply beckons us to follow Him. He asks us to keep His Sabbath-day holy as evidence of our trust in Him.

The Savior longs to see His character reflected in our lives. His desire is for us to uplift Him as our Creator and submit to His will in our lives. When, by God's grace, we do that, we demonstrate to the world our genuine faith in His word. Our obedience to His will is the evidence of our saving relationship with our Creator, Savior and Redeemer. He counsels and assures us, "Let your light so shine before men, that they may see your good works, and glorify your Father which is in heaven" (Matthew 5:16).

Of all the Ten Commandments, none reveals who truly Jesus Christ is as does the Sabbath commandment (Exodus 20:8-11). He is so clearly declared in the Holy Scriptures to be our Creator. He is the one whom we honor by keeping the seventh-day Sabbath. He lovingly bids us, "Come unto me, all ye that labour and are heavy laden, and I will give you rest. Take my yoke upon you and learn of me; for I am meek and lowly in heart: and ye shall find rest unto your souls. For my yoke is easy, and my burden is light" (Matthew 11:28-30).

Therefore, He gave us His Sabbath as a time when we can come apart from the cares of the world and ponder the value, He has placed upon us. That value was made manifest in a place called Calvary where He gave Himself as a ransom to redeem humanity from death.

The Sabbath reminds us that each of us is here for a purpose--to reflect the character of our Lord and Savior, Jesus Christ. It is the enduring pillar of creation and the solid ground of redemption. It is verily the embodiment of salvation truth. The Sabbath is a reminder that we have nothing to offer our Creator save our hearts so He can cleanse them from the sins with which they have been polluted. It is a recurring reminder that appears every seventh day in the annals of Salvation history.

The Sabbath commandment is verily the Creator's seal that authenticates His law. It contains His name (Lord thy God) His title (Creator), and the territory over which He rules (The heaven, the earth, the sea, and all that is in them).

By Hs grace, our lights must shine, as we strive to keep all of His commandments including His Sabbath commandment, thus glorifying our Father which is in heaven. He has encoded His sanctifying principles in His moral law, the Ten Commandments and wants to write them in our hearts. Let us obey them by following our Perfect Example, Jesus Christ, the One who died for you.

Chapter 15

THE PROTEST IS NOT OVER

rotestantism means protesting the un-biblical teachings of the Church of Rome. It is what gave rise to the mighty Protestant Reformation of the 15th, 16th and 17th centuries and birthed the greatest experiment in human civilization, the United States of America. Most of the Christian denominations, which came out of the Papal church in protest of its un-Biblical teachings and man-made traditions, have retained many traits and characteristics of the mother church. Sunday sacredness, in opposition to God's blessed and holy Sabbath-day, is the most prominent. We are cautioned, "It is the spirit of the papacy, the spirit of conformity to worldly customs, the veneration for human traditions above the commandments of God, that is permeating the Protestant churches, and leading them on to do the same work of Sunday exaltation which the papacy has done before them" (Great Controversy, 573, E.G. White).

Today, America, through self-appointed religious leaders, directs the nation back to Rome. Organizations such as the National Back to Church Sunday, the Lord's

Day Alliance, and others, constitute a coalition of Evangelical, Catholic and mainline Sunday-keeping churches who are joining forces for the establishment of Sunday sacredness, not only in America, but around the world. We see the aggressive efforts of organizations such as the European Sun Alliance whose focused purpose is to establish Sunday sacredness throughout the continent. The question is, where are the Protestants?

A great drama is being played out, before our very eyes in these the final hours of earth's history. It revolves around God's word versus the traditions of the papacy. It is the final battle in the Drama of the Ages between the Jesus who died for you and His arch enemy, Satan who wants to destroy you.

The great Protestant Reformer, Martin Luther, along with others such as Calvin, Zwingli, Knox, Edwards, Henry, Clark, Wesley, and Spurgeon, just to name a few, identified the Roman Catholic church as the first beast of Revelation 13 and the papacy as the anti-Christ power of Bible prophecy. As a result of their courage, tens of thousands of Roman Catholics, infected with the holy boldness of those Reformers, returned to the Scriptures and discovered the truth about Jesus. The world has not been the same since.

Luther's 95 Theses which became the foundation of the Protestant Reformation, was quite provocative. It confronted the un-Biblical teachings of the church to which he had dedicated his life, sincerely believing that it was God's church on earth. But, having found the truth and light of God's word, Luther declared, "We are of the conviction that the papacy is the seat of the true and real Antichrist...personally I declare that I owe the pope no other obedience than that of Antichrist..." (Prophetic Faith of Our Fathers, Vol. 1, pg. 121, Froom). His 95 Theses was the beginning of a movement and the engine that drove untold millions to protest against the erroneous dogmas, doctrines, and practices of the Roman Catholic Church.

Unfortunately, today most Protestants and Evangelicals have developed a nauseating case of historical amnesia, all but forgetting the work, commitment, and sacrifice of the Reformers. They have, knowingly or unknowingly, set aside that which distinguishes them from Catholicism, instead joining with her to achieve an un-achievable peace in the name of working for the 'common good'. For the most part, they are oblivious to the conflict in which they are engaged. But all must choose whose which side of the controversy they're on: the God of creation or the papacy's. There is no middle ground.

God is calling His people today to honor Him by keeping all His commandments, including His Sabbath Commandment. Again, Ellen G. White, world renowned Bible commentator, alerts us, "In the movements now in progress in the United States to secure for the institutions and usages of the church the support of the state, Protestants are following in the steps of papists. Nay, more, they are opening the door for the papacy to regain in Protestant America the supremacy which she has lost in the Old World. And that which gives greater significance to this movement is the fact that the principal object contemplated is the enforcement of Sunday observance—a custom which originated with Rome, and which she claims as the sign of her authority" (Great Controversy, pg. 573, E. G. White).

The fact of the matter is that the God of creation has never made Sunday holy. Neither does He force anyone to accept what He offers. Further, legislation of religious dogmas always leads to tyranny and persecution of those who do not agree with the legislated dogma.

We are warned, "The Protestant churches are in great darkness, or they would discern the signs of the times. The Roman Church is employing every device to extend her influence and increase her power in preparation of a fierce and determined conflict to regain control of the world, to re-establish persecution, and undo all that Protestantism has done" (Great Controversy, pg. 565). And what has Protestantism done? It has, above all else, afforded us liberty of conscience, a fundamental principle of the Constitution of the United States of America. But, the Church of Rome hates it with a passion. Pope Pius IX, in his Encyclical Letter of August 15th, 1584, said: "The absurd and erroneous doctrines or ravings in defense of liberty of conscience are a most pestilential error—a pest, of all others, most to be dreaded in a state" Nothing has changed from the perspective of the papal power.

October 31, 1517 was the date. The place was Wittenberg Castle church, Wittenberg, Germany. His name was Martin Luther. Committed to the idea that salvation could be obtained through faith in Jesus Christ alone as a result of God's divine grace only, Luther vigorously objected to the corrupt practice of selling indulgences by the Roman church. Consequently, he defiantly nailed his 95 Theses to the door of the Wittenberg Castle church outlining his discovery of Jesus Christ being the only means of salvation. His singular act is indelibly inscribed in the annals of salvation history as the event that gave birth to the Protestant Reformation. He shook the mediaeval church at its very foundation as thousands fled the church and to find freedom in Christ Jesus.

The Church of Rome responded to Luther's Reformation with its Counter-Reformation. Ignatius Loyola, soldier turned priest and mystical icon, initiated the Jesuit Order, commonly known as the Jesuits. This movement became the most effective and ruthless instrument in the hands of the papacy to overturn and discredit Luther's Reformation. Its objective has always been to undo all that Protestantism has done and to establish the Roman church as the supreme ruler of the world. They are the most formidable foes of the Gospel of Jesus Christ.

So successful has the church's efforts been that Jesuit Pope Francis can announce to the world that the Protest is over. His church, ostensibly commemorating the 500th anniversary of the Protestant Reformation, has drawn almost the entire Protestant church back to her fold. Ironically, it is the pope of Rome and his church that are most proactive in celebrating Luther and commemorating the Protestant Reformation which he ignited. Their celebration, however, is an overmastering deception.

The reality is that they are congratulating themselves on the undeniable effectiveness of Loyola's Counter-Reformation. No one can deny its success; hence their celebration. Francis' joint celebration with the leadership of the Lutheran church in Lund, Sweden on October 31st, 2016 was hailed as a great and memorable moment for Luther's Reformation. Rather, under the pretense of commemorating Martin Luther's Reformation, Francis and his church are announcing to the world that the Church's Counter-Reformation has been undeniably successful--mission accomplished.

The common thread used by the papists to bring Protestants back to the mother church is Sunday sacredness. So, Francis appeals in his Encyclical, LAUDATO SI', "On Sunday, our participation in the Eucharist has special importance. Sunday, like the Jewish Sabbath, is meant to be a day which heals our relationships with God, with ourselves, with others and with the world. Sunday is the day of the Resurrection, the "first day" of the new creation, whose first fruits are the Lord's risen humanity, the pledge of the final transfiguration of all created reality. It also proclaims, "man's eternal rest in God" (LAUDATO SI', Section 237). How can a mere human being transfer the meaning, sacredness, and sanctity of God's Sabbath, the 7th day of the week, to Sunday, the first, and by extension relegate the blessings of the Creator's Jubilee to one he and his church have invented? But this is indeed what Francis has done in LAUDATO SI'.

With bold confidence in the effectiveness of their counter--Reformation program, the Jesuit pope continues the church's long-standing opposition to the God of creation. He is reiterating the position of his predecessors. Thus we find one previous pope declaring, (quoting and earlier pope) "When, through the centuries, she has made laws concerning Sunday rest, the Church has had in mind above all the work of servants and workers, certainly not because this work was any less worthy when compared to the spiritual requirements of Sunday observance, but rather because it needed greater regulation to lighten its burden and thus enable everyone to keep the Lord's Day holy. In this matter, my predecessor Pope Leo XIII in his Encyclical Rerum Novarum spoke of Sunday rest as a worker's right which the State must guarantee" (Pope John Paul 11, Dies Domini, Section 66).

It is past 500 years now and almost all Christendom continue to reject Luther's protest which has affected all of our lives. For, very likely, there would have been no Protestant denomination had not the God of all creation inspired and empowered the humble, God-fearing monk named Martin Luther. He is one of the most influential figures in Western history. This one man's faith in God's word was displayed by his courageous act that changed the course of human history. Luther, by the direction and divine grace of Creator God, discovered that the church he so very much loved was practicing fraud, deception, and treachery beyond his wildest imaginations.

It has not ceased. In the document, From Conflict to Communion, which solidifies the return of the Lutheran church to the Church of Rome and forms the basis for Rome's celebration, this revealing, classical Jesuitical statement is found: "What happened in the past cannot be changed, but what is remembered of the past and how it is remembered can, with the passage of time, indeed change. Remembrance makes the past present. While the past itself is unalterable, the presence of the past in the present is alterable. In view of 2017, the point is not to tell a different history, but to tell that history differently" (From Conflict to Communion, (Ch. 2, Sec 16). In plain language, 'Let us continue to deceive the people'.

How sad that on the 500th anniversary of Luther's potent Protestant Reformation, the church he founded, the Lutherans, have fully clasped hands with the Papal church, effectively agreeing with the current pope that the Protestant Reformation is over. Looking around the religious landscape, one can confidently conclude that many others have agreed with the pope and are following suit. How grieved would Luther and the other Protestant Reformers be could they witness the current rejection of their sacrificial efforts, as millions are embracing popery and returning to the fold of the Roman church? Quite interestingly, none of the doctrines, dogmas, and practices that led to Luther's Protestant Reformation have changed. Those policies resulted in the unmerciful slaughter of tens of millions whose only crime was to choose, like Luther, that salvation is available through Jesus Christ alone. It would therefore not be too difficult to conjecture what will befall those who, like Luther and the other Protestants, continue to reject the spurious teachings of Francis and his church.

Christians everywhere, like the Reformers of old, need to rekindle the spirit of Protestantism and resist Rome's call for universal Sunday sacredness, a tradition contrary to God's commandment which the Roman Church claims is her mark of authority in religious matters. She boasts, "Sunday is our mark of authority...the church is above the Bible, and the transference of Sabbath is proof of that fact." (Catholic Record, Sept 1, 1923). "Perhaps the boldest thing, the most revolutionary change the church ever did happened in the first century. The holy day, the Sabbath, was changed to Sunday...not from any directions noted in Scriptures, but from the church's sense of its own power...People who think that the Scriptures should be the sole authority, should logically become Seventh-day Adventists, and keep Saturday holy"(St. Catherine Church Sentinel, Algonac, Michigan, May 21, 1995).

Rome's Sunday can never accomplish what God's word does in the life of the believer. The Psalmist David assures us, "The law of the Lord is perfect, converting the soul: the testimony of the Lord is sure, making wise the simple. The statutes of the Lord are right, rejoicing the heart: the commandment of the Lord is pure, enlightening the eyes" (Psalms 19:7-8).

As we move beyond the 500th year of Luther's Protest, shamefully, not too many Christians are celebrating the man and his work that paved the way for the liberties we now enjoy. Nevertheless, it is indeed a great mystery that on the anniversary of Luther's courageously monumental act, the professed followers of Jesus Christ would choose, contrary to the word of God, to engage in activities rooted in sorcery, witchcraft and necromancy (Halloween) rather than reflect upon the event that was the foundation for their civil and religious liberty. Why would they choose carving pumpkins and pretending to be ghosts instead of praising the God of all creation for sending Luther and the other reformers, many of whom gave their lives, so that we can live and enjoy the freedoms we do today?

Contrary to Rome's attempt to influence the world otherwise, the Protest is not over. The Jesus who died for you is the foundation upon which your faith must rest. He declares that the protest is alive and well. Says He, "If ye keep my commandments, ye shall abide in my love; even as I have kept my Father's commandments and abide in his love" (John 15:10). By God's grace, be part of the protest and obey the one who died for you.

Chapter 16

AMAZING GRACE

$\mathscr{I}$t was in the midst of a twelve year plus crack cocaine addiction that an associate of mine remarked to me, "You don't need money...you need Jesus". Upon hearing those words, I thought that it was the most unkind and terrible thing Captain Medas could have said to me. I came to him penniless, homeless, and expected that he would show a bit of sympathy towards me and loan me some money. In retrospect, those were indeed the best words he could have said to me.

It hadn't been very long before that I was evicted from my modest one-bedroom apartment and had my belongings stored at Medas's warehouse where he ran a shipping company in Brooklyn, New York. I was very grateful for him not charging me any monies for storing my furniture and other household items at his warehouse. I had become familiar with Captain Medas in the process of publishing and marketing a magazine targeted to the Caribbean community in the United States. He was a supporter of the magazine and had placed some advertising with it. Our relationship had been one of professional friendship. Coming to him to 'borrow' a few dollars was quite out of the ordinary. He was no doubt aware of that fact.

As I made my request, he looked at me, eyeball to eyeball, and asked a very poignant question, "Aubrey, do you use drugs?" To which I boldly responded, "NO". Of course, I was lying. More likely than not, had he given me any money, I would have put it in the crack cocaine pipe. It must have been his spiritual discernment that caused him to ask me such a question. The old sea captain was a religious man and an elder in his church. In reflecting upon his response to my request for money with an invitation to come to Jesus and visit his church was one of those moments of divine destiny that I did not immediately recognized.

Mine was not in any way a conscious response to the call of Jesus on my life; but rather out of my respect for and admiration of Captain Medas, I accepted his invitation to visit his church. His invitation evoked a double surprise. First, I was not brought up in a religious home, so going to church was a brand-new experience for me. Secondly, I was quite surprised when the captain told me that his church met on Saturdays. I, like most of the people I knew, thought that going to church on Sunday was the right, God-ordained thing to do. Upon visiting his church a few weeks later, I found the members to be quite loving and accepting of me. I would continue to visit sporadically as I struggled with my crack cocaine addiction which remained the driving force in my life.

On one particular Sabbath morning, following a rather eventful and unforgettable Friday night of uncontrollable crack-cocaine use, I felt not only compelled, but propelled to go to his church. I realized that I had not taken my clothes out of the cleaners as I normally would do on Friday afternoons. Besides, I didn't have much clothes since most of my money was consumed in the crack cocaine pipe. My slacks and jacket that I wore the previous day were sweaty and rumpled. I reached for an old sweater and a pair of blue jeans. I quickly got dressed, washed my face, combed my hair, brushed my teeth, grabbed my big white Bible, and started out to church. It never occurred to me what anyone might say when they saw me in this condition at church. On my previous visits, I was quite 'appropriately' attired, displaying my Dr. Jekyll persona. But this was Mr. Hyde.

The church was about three or more miles from where I lived. I had no money left over after a night of incessant crack cocaine use; but God had told me, "Go to church". I had bought my big white Bible for $2.00 from a roadside vendor in downtown Brooklyn, New York some years ago. It was a King James Version. It was about twelve inches long and ten inches wide and three inches thick. In addition to the Scriptures, it contained lots of resourceful information. I read it as often as I could but never quite saw the message of salvation in Jesus Christ.

Reading my Bible was simply an intellectual exercise more than anything else. As I started out to Medas' church that Sabbath morning, I was sweating even more profusely than the night before. The junkie, Mr. Hyde persona, was present but I kept on going. I was paranoid yet deeply self-conscious of my despicable physical condition.

As I arrived at the church, I could sense that everyone, from the greeters to my friend Medas detected that something was strangely different about me. The welcome was not as warm and friendly as it had been in the past. Some stared at me as though I was a creature from another planet. It was evident that in their minds, I was out of place. None of it mattered to me. After the night I had just gone through, I was simply so happy to be alive and wanted only to hear a word from the Lord. I was convinced that if there was ever a time, I needed God, it was then.

It was a little passed eleven thirty o'clock when I arrived at church. Dr. Jeffries, the church's charismatic, passionate pastor had just begun to preach. In his usual animated, dramatic and engaging style, he was talking about who man is and what is his true relationship to God. He had a life size mirror as a prop on the platform as he dramatized how man was created in the image of God. I was no Bible student; however, what he was saying seemed to be tailor made for me. I walked to the very front of the church and sat on the second row on the right side of the sanctuary. I knew I was a spectacle but that had not mattered at all to me. I was simply thankful to be alive.

Pastor Jeffries obviously noticed my strange condition, but I could see no indication that he resented or was otherwise displeased with me. He kept on preaching and I listened most attentively. After a short while I felt relaxed, forgetting about my present condition and the events of the previous night. Based upon his presentation, I began to meditate upon who God is, who I am, and what is my relationship is to Him. Despite my circumstances, I had never felt this valuable in my life before. Dr. Jeffries looked directly into my eyes on several occasions as he brought home the point of what man can be in Jesus Christ. I don't remember his Scripture texts, but the message was clear...you are valuable to God. That moment is inevitably etched on my mind. It was the moment I began consciously focus on the mercy of God and His love for me.

At the end of the meeting, the good pastor descended from the platform and came directly over to where I was sitting. He gave me a most penetrating stare, an iron-clad handshake, and simply asked, "How are you". I humbly replied, "I am fine, sir". He gave me the brightest smile imaginable and moved on to exit the sanctuary leading the processional. His actions spoke louder to my ears than any words he uttered that morning. It said to me that I am somebody, God loves me and so did he. I felt the touch of God's amazing grace and unfathomable love through Pastor Jeffries.

I hurried out of the church not stopping to say anything to anybody except a passing hello. It was in the middle of summer and the temperature was very hot, perhaps ninety degrees or more. I started my journey back to my apartment, again sweating profusely, but this time thanking God for speaking so clearly and directly to me. I meditated on my experience of the previous night. I thought on how close I had come to dying and how God had spared my life. I contemplated the message from Dr. Jeffries and how it spoke to me personally. I reflected on the stare, the handshake and smile he gave me. My mind reflected on the religious classes I had to take during my high school years in my native country of Guyana, South America. Those lessons now began to make sense to me.

Beyond those religious classes I had taken in high school, my conscious religious experience had been almost nonexistent. Before visiting Dr. Jeffries' church, I had not attended a church service since I was about ten or eleven years old. My experience on that almost fatal night taught me that I can call out to my Father and that He will hear and answer. I knew very little of my Heavenly Father and much less of how to relate to Him. I always kept my big white Bible on my dining room table located just inside my apartment door. It was filled with colorful maps of the Bible lands. It contained helpful, easy to understand study guides of the great

themes of the Bible. I read it whenever I was sober
enough to do so. It never occurred to me that God was
moving in my life to draw me ever closer to Him. I later
was convicted that my Father had led me to that Bible.
Having had that experience, I began to take a closer,
more conscious look into its sacred pages.

As I perused my coveted Bible, my thoughts would
take me to the Bible lands. My mind was being
impressed with the unfathomable love of God and the
grand theme of salvation for men's souls. As I read the
life of Jesus, I began to see not only the great love that
God has for the human race; but my eyes were opened to
the lengths to which He would go to save a sinner like
me. I began to experience the great joy, peace and
comfort that Jesus' love brings to men's hearts. I was
especially impressed with His parables in a very
endearing way. Though I did not grasp their full
meaning, I was intrigued by what a great storyteller
Jesus was. He would take the most complex issues and
through a simple story made it plain so that the smallest
child, the unlearned and uneducated could understand.
Imperceptibly, but surely, I was being drawn to my
Savior. He was verily delivering me from the enemy's
grasp. It was not as if I was intentionally seeking to know
God in a deliberate way; rather I was simply attracted to
the Bible and the story of Jesus.

As I reflect upon those experiences, I realize that
God was not only drawing me closer to Him; but He was
preparing me to become an ambassador for Him. I had

no human Bible instructor, but by His Holy Spirit, I was being enlightened and edified in the magnitude of His love for me and all humanity.

My rather increasing personal Bible Studies were supplemented by my tuning in to some of the popular televangelists. I thought that they were so dynamic, charismatic and knowledgeable. But both the Cross of Calvary and God's Seventh-day Sabbath were missing from their presentations. It hadn't occurred to me at that time how important those were to my salvation. My personal studies and attendance at Pastor F.E. Roy Jeffries church had convinced me beyond the shadow of any doubt of the value of Calvary and the soundness and validity of God' Seventh-day Sabbath. There would be a great conflict in my mind as I would get high on crack cocaine on Friday nights, and at the same time thinking it was God's Sabbath day. It was a great struggle for me. I knew not only that doing crack was wrong; but by engaging on such activities on God's holy Sabbath was doubly dangerous. In the process, I was experiencing His patience and longsuffering with me. I pondered? How could He still love me?

My use of crack cocaine continued to haunt me. Nevertheless, I was finding more time to read my beautiful big, white Bible. I was being transformed by His grace.

From more than a twelve-year plus addiction to crack cocaine, estrangement from family, licentious living and near-death experiences, God has delivered me. He has moved me from the crack house to His house. He has restored my mind and has equipped me to tell men and women of His boundless love, unfathomable mercy and amazing grace. I have experienced His grace to pardon, transform, and empower to keep His law, including His Seventh-day Sabbath commandment.

Not only has He enlisted me for the position of ambassador; He has paid my wages two thousand years before I accepted the assignment. He paid it at a place called Calvary. There He gave the ultimate price for my ambassadorship. He gave His life in the person of His Son, my Savior and elder brother, Jesus Christ. The cruel cross of Calvary upon which He made the payment for my ambassadorship is God's object lesson illustrating to the world the cost of sin and the price of redemption for sinners like me.

My Lord and Savior Jesus Christ, who knew no sin, became sin for me that I may become righteous in Him. He took upon Him my transgressions in which He had no part; so that I may obtain salvation which I do not deserve. This is a great mystery that my feeble, finite mind cannot and perhaps may never fully comprehend.

In my walk from crack to Christ, I made some amazing discoveries. It was revealed to me that as I dwell upon the life of Jesus, my character was being transformed to become more like His. As I contemplate His payment on Calvary, my pride was turned into humility. My drug addiction to crack cocaine and drunkenness were remade into sobriety as I beheld His glory and majesty. I became addicted to the Gospel. Selfishness and other rough traits of my personality have been turned into attitudes of kindness, benevolence and politeness by partaking of His amazing grace. In the light of His love and mercy towards me, my prejudices were dispossessed and were replaced by love, respect and appreciation for all my fellow men. I was made to realize that it was not the qualification of the applicant that mattered; but rather that the position qualifies the applicant. Coming to acknowledge and obeying, by His grace, all His commandments, including, His seventh-day Sabbath commandment is part of that qualifying.

He is waiting to qualify you today. My story, a glimpse of which I just shared with you, is a testimony of God's amazing grace. It is the evidence of that His grace which not only transforms but empowers us to keep all His commandments. Mine is the report one man's encounter with the One and Only true God, the God of creation and recreation. He is the One who gave us the Sabbath as a sign between Him and us.

I have proven by experience what my favorite Bible commentator has to say about His autobiographical record. "The central theme of the Bible, the theme about which every other in the whole book clusters, is the redemption plan, the restoration in the human soul of the image of God. From the first intimation of hope in the sentence pronounced in Eden to that last glorious promise of the Revelation, "They shall see His face; and His name shall be in their foreheads" (Revelation 22:4), the burden of every book and every passage of the Bible is the unfolding of this wondrous theme,—man's uplifting,—the power of God, "which giveth us the victory through our Lord Jesus Christ." 1 Corinthians 15:57. (Education pg. 125, E.G. White).

God is no respecter of persons. As He has done with me, He will do for and with you. I invite you to taste of His Amazing Grace. He is Jesus, the One that is revealed from Genesis to Revelation. He is the One that died for you.

Other Books By This Author

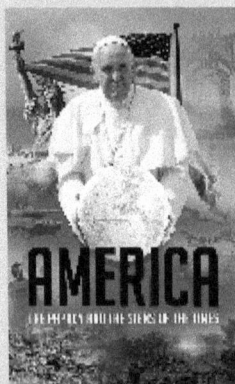

While many are wondering about, yea speculating, even denying America's role in Bible Prophecy, the nation is rapidly marching towards its prophetic destiny. The book, **America, the Papacy and the Signs of the Times**, gives the true picture of the United States in Bible Prophecy. Though many deny America's place in End-Time prophecy, this volume shows that undoubtedly, not only is the United States featured in Bible Prophecy, but meticulously reveals its critical role in the closing scenes of earth's history.

Order your copy today (Postage included) $12.95

Today, there is much discussion in Christendom as to what day is God's Sabbath. Is it Sunday, the first day of the week; or is it Saturday, the seventh? Does it really matter, anyway? The book, **God's Sabbath Truth...a decision to make**, provides all the answers from the perspectives of the Bible, history and contemporary world affairs. It traces God's Sabbath from creation to the day in which we live. The Book answers the most popular questions that many have about God's Sabbath and its place in our lives.

Order your copy today (Postage included) $14.95

To order, visit our website www.adventtruth.org
Or send check or money order to:
Advent Truth Ministries
P.O. Box 307, Forsyth, GA 31029

www.ingramcontent.com/pod-product-compliance
Lightning Source LLC
Chambersburg PA
CBHW060242050426

42448CB00009B/1562